Listen to the Mocking Bird

By S. J. PERELMAN

"The grift has a gentle touch."—D. W. MAURER, THE BIG CON

DRAWINGS BY HIRSCHFELD

Simon and Schuster • New York

All of the pieces in this book originally
appeared in the *New Yorker*.

PUBLISHED BY SIMON AND SCHUSTER
ROCKEFELLER CENTER, 630 FIFTH AVENUE
NEW YORK, NEW YORK 10020

FIRST SIMON AND SCHUSTER PAPERBACK PRINTING 1970

SBN 671-20718-0
MANUFACTURED IN THE UNITED STATES OF AMERICA

For Marion Dorn and E. McKnight Kauffer

CONTENTS

The Sweeter the Tooth, the Nearer the Couch

I T MUST have been about ten days after my arrival on the island of Penang, in British Malaya, that I first became positive I was talking to myself. The realization dawned on me at four-thirty one afternoon as I was seated in a room at the Western & Occidental Hotel examining the tea tray the native boy had just left. On it was the same everlasting finger banana and potted-meat sandwich he had been bringing me every morning and afternoon for the past week. "Finger bananas and potted-meat sandwiches," I suddenly heard myself say in a strained, furious voice. "Potted-meat sandwiches and finger bananas. So that's what you came all the way to the storied East for — to sit in this benighted, pestilential hole reading Penguin reprints and eating potted-meat sandwiches. And now," I went on bitterly, "you're talking to yourself to boot. Nice going. Keep on this way, lover, and the next thing you know, you'll be running amok with a kris in your teeth."

The conviction that I was batting a very sticky wicket had, as a matter of fact, been growing steadily in me almost from the moment I had set foot on the island. Penang (unless it has since sunk into the sea without leaving a trace, a thought that fills me with equanimity) lies off the Malayan coastline twenty-four hours northwest of Singapore. In a moment of aberration, I had proceeded from Siam to Penang, assured by everyone that I could expect an idyllic interlude there before going on to Ceylon on the steamer due within the fort-night. I found that at least two of the claims my informants had made for Penang were accurate. Its beaches *were* the equal of any in the South Seas, and, they should have added, equally accessible. The food at the Western & Occidental was indeed as good as that of the Raffles in Singapore, and a more ambiguous compliment is hardly conceivable. Both establishments served a variety of fried bread that melted in the mouth, fusing your inlays with it. In the hands of their chefs, the mango lost none of its unique aromatic flavor, and to any-one who loves kerosene there can be no warmer tribute.

After a trip — freely punctuated with nosebleeds — up the funicular railway, a visit to a couple of sleazy dance halls full of overwrought fifteen-year-old Malay jitterbugs, and a hike through the botanical gardens culminating in a painful bite from a parakeet, I decided I had had a plethora of sightseeing and badly needed the society of Europeans. The only ones in evidence were the British civil servants in the hotel lobby glowering into their gin pahits and gimlets and explaining to each other that the Nips had captured Singapore by trickery. My tentative efforts to fraternize with them quickly defined the status of the American tourist in Penang. "The cheek of that beggar!" I overheard a scarlet-faced bureaucrat exploding when he thought I was out of earshot. "Did you see him cotton up to me with that smarmy smile?" His companion shook his head commiseratingly. It always happened when you let these Yankees in, he said. Nothing but a pack of cardsharps and blacklegs. The whole tone of the place went to the demnition bow-wows.

It was on the twenty-third of May, however, that the real nightmare began — the chain of afflictions that determined me to restrict my future tropical travel to a tufted ottoman and the pages of Somerset Maugham. I remember the date because it was my wife's birthday, and, having sent off a congratulatory cable collect, I threw down an extra peg in her honor before dinner. It was just as well I did, for it helped anesthetize me to a meal that would have touched off a mutiny in the hulks at Portsmouth. I struggled inadequately with a viscous chlorinated soup, filet of squid basted with lard, and a dollop of tapioca awash in sorghum, and then, sore in spirit, plodded out into the town, desperate for some way to occupy the hours until bedtime. The prospect of seeing either of the two Tarzan films was insupportable, especially as I had seen them twice already — on the two previous evenings — and my knowledge of the Hokkien dialect was too rudimentary to enable me to appreciate the Chinese ritual play at the New World amusement park.

I had been drifting about aimlessly for over an hour, gaping at the fighting fish in the pet shops and watching the rattan weavers plait their baskets, when an overwhelming urge for candy gripped me. Now, I am perfectly aware what scorn a confession of this sort may arouse; a passion for sweets has subjected me for years to the derision of friends and family alike. Notwithstanding, at the risk of being classed as a leper, I can envisage circumstances under which one might prefer a peanut cluster to a pony of armagnac, when the craving for a caramel can become so keen as to amount to an obsession. That evening in the Penang Road was one of those occasions. I knew that unless I came by a gumdrop or a bit of licorice forthwith, it was good-by Charlie. Short of murder, there were no lengths I was unprepared to go to for a piece of candy, and if murder was unavoidable, I was not going to let mere squeamishness stand in my way.

Luckily, nothing quite so drastic was necessary; scarcely fifty yards away was a fine confectionery store, loaded with all manner of goodies and run by an extremely obliging Chinese. Through whatever devious black-market channels, he had procured a supply of Swiss bitter chocolate, a delicacy esteemed by connoisseurs above white jade, and ten times as rare in the Orient. Purely as a stopgap, I purchased two economy-size bars, half a pound each of peanut brittle and crystallized ginger, and a dozen caraway cookies, and, assuring the proprietor that I would return the next day to lay in a real stock if they proved satisfactory, sprinted back to my room. I would have preferred to hold my debauch elsewhere than under a mosquito netting that

3

kept entangling itself in the peanut brittle, but except for the light by the bed the room was bathed in dense shadow, and a man is entitled to see what he is eating. Nevertheless, and despite an uncomfortable suspicion that the affair was akin to a dormitory revel, it was a deeply satisfying experience, and conscious for the first time since landing on Penang of a measure of contentment, I fell asleep.

My serenity was short-lived. The next morning at seven-thirty, as I sat up in bed gulping down the perpetual tea, potted-meat sandwich, and banana, I noticed a fuzzy, darkish line vibrating across the floor from the windows to the dresser. I dismissed it as some trifling myopia caused by my gluttony of the night before, but when it was still there an hour later, an obscure disquietude stole over me. It turned to horror when I investigated the bag of sweets I had left lying open on the dresser top. Swarms of tiny red ants were churning through the candy, purloining huge fragments of ginger and chocolate. Leaning perilously over the window sill, I could see their caravan extending three stories up the façade of the building, right to my quarters. In the first access of panic, I went numb. It seemed futile to join battle with an enemy numbering into the millions, whose patience was proverbial and who knew the local terrain so much better than I. Then a cold fury possessed me. Nobody was going to deprive me of the one consolation I had found in this miserable backwater; I'd show the little red devils what American know-how is capable of under pressure. "Think you can bulldoze me, do you?" I cried. "Well, you wait, my friends. I've got a couple of tricks up my sleeve you never heard of, and, what's more, I have not yet begun to fight!"

By dint of searching over half of Penang that afternoon, I finally located a tinsmith's shop, where I bought a metal box about six inches long and four deep. It had a tight-fitting cover I was sure would exclude any marauders, but to make doubly certain I also provided myself with a roll of rubber bicycle tape. The Chinese candy merchant started making obeisances a full block away as I approached his bazaar. Though he exerted every possible blandishment,

I waved aside the assortment of lozenges, lollipops, and peppermints he had prepared and bade him fill the box with a duplicate of my previous purchase.

If a single ant remained in my bedchamber when I got back to it, the sharp eye of the room boy had overlooked it. A penetrating odor of disinfectant hung over everything, including, to my particular chagrin, the mosquito netting, so that my bedtime snack lost some of its savor. This was compensated for, however, by the triumph I felt as I sealed the box with the rubber tape and concealed it in a dresser drawer before turning in. Maybe I wasn't pukka enough for those stuffed shirts in the lobby, I chuckled, but I could teach them a thing or two about ants.

My house of cards tumbled abruptly when I got up the following morning. Not only were the poachers back but they had insinuated themselves into the drawer and were rifling the box with complete contempt for the lid and the rubber tape. Their persistence might have moved me to admiration had I not been so thoroughly enraged. Apart from the shock to my vanity, it was clear a way must be found to circumvent them before they bankrupted me. At length, I hit on a solution that should have occurred to me earlier. There was one barrier they could never breach — a good, lethal insect powder. That night, equipped with a totally fresh batch of candy and a can of ten-per-cent DDT, I took special pains to render the box impregnable. I crisscrossed it with tape, sprinkled a moat of DDT around it, sealed the drawer itself with tape, and dusted the powder along the route the ants had followed. My slumber was chaotic and intermittent; twice I got up to reconnoiter, the second time just prior to dawn, but there was no sign of them. I sank back into bed suffused with an overpowering sense of relief. However costly the contest had been in self-esteem and nervous strength, victory was mine at last.

I pray I shall never again suffer the anguish I experienced when I opened my eyes and beheld the blurred, wavering column pulsating across the floor and up the front of the dresser. None of my obstacles had retarded the creatures in the slightest; on the contrary, to judge from their vigor and increased number, the DDT had stimulated them and whetted their appetite. They scurried in and out of the drawer, singing chanteys as they worked, pausing only to thumb their noses jeeringly in my direction. By the time the boy padded in with the tea, the sandwich, and the banana, I had recovered sufficient aplomb to consider the situation with some degree of detachment. I hesitated to employ the one remaining arrow in my quiver, and yet to quit Penang knowing I had been worsted by both man and beast would throw a pall over the rest of my journey. Using bribery and every scrap of pidgin I could muster, I explained to the boy that I wished a set of glass casters filled with gasoline placed under the legs of the dresser. The smirk that invaded his face clearly betrayed his opinion of white eccentricity and I could tell there would be high hilarity belowstairs, but I was hardly in a position to take umbrage. At the candy shop, buying the same merchandise the fourth day in a row, I cloaked my humiliation with an unnecessary display of brusqueness. Significantly enough, the sweetmeats no longer inflamed me as they had; in fact, I had difficulty in repressing a shudder when the storekeeper invited me to try a coconut bar on the house, an offer that formerly would have brought the roses to my cheeks. On the way back to the hotel I filled in the keystone of the arch; I stopped in at the chemist's and bought a quart jar of ant paste.

What the final outcome was, unfortunately, will have to remain a secret until I revisit Penang, which I plan to do the week of the millennium. Just before dinner that evening, as I was smearing ant paste on the candy and taping the entire front of the dresser, talking away to myself thirteen to the dozen, the desk clerk telephoned. My ship was in the harbor and was due to sail in two hours. He was afraid, he said anxiously, that I might have trouble getting aboard on such short notice. No fears were ever less well founded. Fifteen minutes later, a jagged flash, described by some as Halley's comet and by others as an ecstatic American bearing satchels, mo-

*. . . The DDT had stimulated
them and whetted their appetite.*

mentarily lit up the portico of the Western & Occidental Hotel and
disappeared in the direction of the waterfront. I gave the room boy
five Straits dollars and a Bombay mail address to let me know what
he found in 318 the next morning, but I never heard from him. Beggar
probably ate the candy, ant paste and all. That's the trouble with
those natives — you can't depend on them. Pack of lazy, good-for-
nothing loafers; if it weren't for our chaps out there, the whole lot'd
go to the demnition bow-wows. And this isn't hearsay, mind you.
I've seen the thing with my own eyes.

Mortar and Pestle

SCENE: The office of Bruce Hyssop, general manager of the Condor Pharmacies, a chain of Los Angeles drugstores. This is a handsome oval room sixty feet long with spun-glass fiber walls, carpeted in Turkey-red vicuña; from the production standpoint, a ruinously expensive set which would tax the facilities of the Radio City Music Hall or La Scala in Milan, but don't let's start by pinching pennies. At center, strung from the ceiling by two wires of unequal length, is the executive's nonobjective desk, a vast slab of Philippine mahogany that vibrates capriciously at the slightest touch. Since it contains no drawers and its surface is so tilted that pencils and mail promptly slide off, its value is debatable, but not with Hyssop, who conceived it and whose arrival is momentarily expected as the curtain rises. Facing the desk, and exquisitely uncomfortable in their nonrepresentational chairs, are three of his lieutenants — Swickard, Thimig, and Miss Fackenthal.

MISS FACKENTHAL: You really ought to try their food, Cyprian. That is, if you like something on the unusual side.

SWICKARD: What's the name of it again?

MISS F.: Frenzi's Fish Grotto. It's out in North Hollywood, just this side of that big musical hypodermic that advertises the hospital plan.

THIMIG: Oh, yes, I've seen it. It's shaped like a casserole.

MISS F.: No, it's shaped like a restaurant. It's a kind of novel idea.

SWICKARD: Say, that's a new twist. Food's good, eh?

MISS F.: Yummy. They take these big Idaho potatoes — honestly, they're almost two feet long — scoop out the inside, and fill them with macaroni. You'd swear you were eating potatoes.

THIMIG: What do they do with the part they scoop out?

MISS F.: They serve it in an eggnog with sour cream, and it's simply heavenly. Ricky and I were so full by the time we got to the Friendly Fevers we could hardly climb up into our trays.

SWICKARD: I've always meant to drop into that fever spot. A lot of picture people go there, I understand.

MISS F.: It's packed. Lauren Bacall's cousin was right in the next oven to me, and she was so gracious and democratic, she couldn't be sweeter. Believe me, when they finish baking out the fatigue, you haven't got a nerve left in your body. And *hungry!* On the way home, we stopped at a Chinese drive-in and had two whole dishes of pork fooyoung.

SWICKARD: Sounds first-rate, Thimig. Let's make up a party some night.

THIMIG: Well, Bedraglia and I haven't stepped out much since we bought our ranch in the Valley. She likes to stick pretty close to her ouija board, you know, and after I rake up the grounds, it's practically bedtime.

SWICKARD: Seems to me you spend half your life raking that place.

THIMIG: I have to. There's an apricot ranch alongside us, and the fruit keeps piling up in our patio and attracting flies.

MISS F.: That's the trouble with those small ranches. You don't have any privacy.

THIMIG: No, ours is good-sized. We've got a forty-foot frontage. But it's the incinerator that makes the property. You'll have to come out some Sunday and taste our ribs.

SWICKARD: How do you fix them?

THIMIG: It's very simple. All you do is mix the barbecue sauce, paint it on, and then, when it's almost dry, lick it off. We got the recipe from an old Spanish hidalgo in Santa Monica.

MISS F.: Gee, I wonder what's holding up Mr. Hyssop. He's usually on the dot.

THIMIG: He went over to inspect the new store in Pasadena. Probably delayed in traffic.

SWICKARD: I wish he'd get a move on. I was planning to have my blood pressure tested before lunch.

THIMIG: Where do you go? Over on South Hill Street?

SWICKARD: Yes, the open-air stand across from where they sell the goat glands. They charge a quarter, but they validate your parking check.

THIMIG: A *quarter?* Most of them do it for fifteen cents.

SWICKARD: Listen, brother, it doesn't pay to skimp on your health. So it costs a little extra; at least you know where you stand. (*Hyssop enters, petulance visible on his plump, sallow face. His aides greet him deferentially.*)

OMNES: How did the sneak preview go last night, B. H.? Did we get a hand on the citrate of magnesia? How many bolts of linoleum did we sell?

HYSSOP (*frowning*):It needs work. From the reaction cards, it looks as if my hunch were right. The average public isn't ready for phone booths in the front of the store.

SWICKARD: Remember my prediction, Bruce? I said it would confuse them!

THIMIG: I experienced dubiety anent it, too. You've got to hide telephones in the back, among the cigarette cartons.

MISS F.: Or down a good, dark stairway, so you can use a neon arrow. Dramatize it — appeal to their sense of adventure, of the unknown.

HYSSOP (*nodding*): Correct. Now, myself, I like the front of our stores kept severe, even a shade Spartan. Just a few airplane tires on a counter, some electric pads, money belts, facial tissues, or so. That whets people's interest and tempts them to browse. (*They all vigorously echo his sentiments. Meanwhile, the desk before him sways erratically, dumping the papers and fountain pen he has placed on it on the floor. As Swickard and Thimig scramble to retrieve them, Hyssop's brow darkens.*) Have any of you been fiddling with these wires?

"What's that? Aren't you satisfied with our Southern-California climate?"

THIMIG: Gosh, no, Bruce! (*Unthinking.*) You see, the damp weather causes them to expand and contract, and consequently —

HYSSOP (*instantly*): What's that? Aren't you satisfied with our southern-California climate?

THIMIG (*anguished*): Me? I'm wild about it! I'd rather be dead here than alive in Cedar Rapids — you know that, Bruce!

HYSSOP: You're an Easterner, Thimig. Sooner or later, they always sell you out. (*Thimig demonstrates his loyalty by producing an aerial view of Cedar Rapids, tearing it to shreds, and grinding them under his heel. Hyssop relents.*) All right, but better watch your step hereafter. Well, let's hear the weekly suggestions. Anything promising come in?

Miss F.: There's one from the manager of the Beverly Hills branch. They get a studio-type clientele, mostly, in their fountain, individuals with an acid condition and nervous indigestion.

Hyssop (*impatiently*): We went into all that last fall. It isn't feasible to spray the customers with cocaine.

Miss F.: No, this is another approach. He says why not add pepsin to some of the ready dishes and feature a line of heartburn specials.

Hyssop: There's no royal road to stomach relief. Seymour Erstweil is a real go-getter, but he doesn't grasp the basic psychology. The patron *wants* to feel distress coming on, so he can counteract it with the proper medication. Take that away and half the pleasure of eating is gone. You follow?

Swickard: I never thought it through before, but you've put your finger on the crux of the matter.

Thimig (*sotto voce*): Has that man got a gift for congealing the whole thing in a nutshell! It's spooky.

Hyssop (*modestly*): My mind runs that way. Ever since I'm a tad, why, I've had a restless impulse to probe beneath the surface, to constantly analyze, analyze, analyze.

Swickard: Which it's the hallmark of every industrial wizard worth a hoot.

Thimig: You can say *that* again. (*Swickard starts to say it again, trails off as Hyssop rises and stands plunged in thought.*)

Hyssop: For instance, the lighting in our stores. I don't know what's wrong, but the clerks still look too normal. They're not waxy enough.

Miss F.: We installed the pistachio-tinted bulbs you wanted.

Hyssop: Uh-uh, it's a sort of a phosphorescent glow in their skins that I'm after. Unearthly, so to speak.

Thimig: Would it help any to pipe in organ recitals? Maybe if we slowed down the tempo, we'd get a more trancelike effect.

Hyssop: No, I guess I'm just reaching for the moon. I only cite this as an example of how the over-all organization could be improved. You can't be petty. You've got to set new horizons on your thinking.

I believe Swickard made the point a moment ago that my attack was global. That pleased me.

SWICKARD (*blushing with pleasure*): Thanks, Bruce. In line with that, I've been cuddling my wits for some solution as regards our triple-decker sandwiches. Why can't we make the doily an essential part of the whole, thus luring the diner to consume it along with his repast?

HYSSOP: By George, I think you're on the right track. An edible doily.

SWICKARD: Made out of the same brake lining we use for the toast and the filling. That way, we wouldn't sacrifice the ungainliness we have to retain and there wouldn't be any disgusting leftovers on the dish.

HYSSOP: You've got an exciting notion there, Swickard, but it's earthbound. The plate should be edible too.

THIMIG: And the forks, and the spoons! Why not the whole fountain?

HYSSOP: No, no. One thing at a time. It's vital to keep a line of demarcation between the food and the fixtures.

THIMIG: I was just trying to think globally, Bruce.

HYSSOP: I'll take up the plate idea with the lab. It mustn't be too tasty; it should duplicate the cardboard flavor of the plates we're using at present. Now, was there anything else?

MISS F.: Well, B. H., I've had my ear to the ground lately and I hear a lot of criticism of our soda dispensers. Everyone says they look drab.

HYSSOP: I thought I gave orders to put epaulets and frogs on their tunics.

MISS F.: We did. We even changed their forage caps to bearskins like the Coldstream Guards wear, but the novelty wore off and the patrons are muttering again.

SWICKARD: Boss, can I voice a proposal that it might floor you with its boldness, albeit it's freighted with the germ of an arresting idea?

HYSSOP (*joining his fingertips*): Sketch in the outlines, however nebulous.

SWICKARD: Why not caparison our dispensers in a different costume each week, so as to typify various current fiestas and sports events in the public eye?

HYSSOP: Hm-m. It's a meaty concept. You mean like during the Rose Bowl tourney they would be accoutered in nose guards and moleskins, during the Santa Ana baby parade in rompers and bibs, and so forth?

SWICKARD: Yes, only made out of crepe paper in attractive pastel shades; viz., orange, lilac, and puce. Can you visualize how that would pep up the personnel if bathed in a pink spotlight to boot?

HYSSOP: I like it, Swickard. There's a nice lilt to it. Naturally, it's a speck humdrum as it stands — we've got to put wings on it — but it's a beginning. You agree, Miss Fackenthal?

MISS F.: Bruce, I'm crazy for it. Speaking as a woman, it slakes my feminine thirst for color.

THIMIG: Personally, I'd like to see it carried over into the drug department, too. Couldn't our pharmacists wear a conical hat like Nostradamus — you know, embroidered with planets and signs of the zodiac?

HYSSOP (*dangerously*): Why don't you go the whole hog, Thimig? Maybe you'd like us to fill our prescriptions with newts and salamanders.

THIMIG (*involuntarily*): They'd probably do the trick as well as those pills and powders we stock. (*He turns deadly pale as Hyssop's eyes bore into him.*) That is, I mean —

HYSSOP: Yes? Was there something you wished to add?

THIMIG: No, I — er — I was just thinking of the spirit message my wife got the other night. It said a change was impending. I — guess she meant a change of garb.

HYSSOP: That depends on how you interpret it. (*Swickard and Miss Fackenthal fade swiftly out. Hyssop's smile gleams like a scimitar and his voice sinks to a coo; his morning is made.*) You know, Thimig, for some time now I've had the feeling you were homesick for Cedar Rapids.

CURTAIN

Don't Bring Me Oscars
(When It's Shoesies That I Need)

IS THERE anybody hereabouts who would like to pick up, absolutely free, the exclusive American rights to one of the most
thrilling documentary films ever left unfinished? I know where such
a property can be acquired, together with the exclusive world-wide
rights, a brand-new Bell & Howell camera, a director's whistle, a
folding canvas chair (my name can always be painted out and your
own substituted), a pair of white riding breeches, and a megaphone
for barking orders at actors. In fact, I am even prepared to slip a deuce
to anyone who removes a bundle containing the foregoing from my
flat, and, what's more, I'll throw in the issue of the *Times* that inspired the whole business.

The impulse to capture on film a small but significant segment of
the life around me was awakened by a feature article, in the Sunday
screen section of that paper, on Roberto Rossellini. "Armed only with
a movie camera and an idea," reported a Berlin correspondent, "the
gifted director of *Open City* and *Paisan* has been shooting a picture
called *Berlin, Year Zero*, with a nonprofessional cast headed by an
eleven-year-old street urchin." It was the account of Rossellini's icono-
clastic production technique that particularly riveted my attention:

The script is literally being written as the shooting progresses in an
effort to keep it as realistic as possible. When young Edmund, the star, is
in a dramatic situation, Rossellini asks, "What would you say if this really

15

happened to you?" The boy comes back with some vivid remark which probably would not get by the Eric Johnston office and if it isn't too obscene it goes into the script. Once during a street scene a truckload of bread went by. Forgetting everything, Edmund piped, "My goodness, I could eat all that bread!" "Don't cut, don't cut!" shouted Rosellini. "Leave it in!"

The unabashed, Rabelaisian coarseness of Edmund's remark understandably brought a tide of crimson to my cheeks, but when the shock had subsided, it presented a challenge. If Edmund's exclamation was dramatic, the casual dialogue around my own household was pure Ibsen. For all I knew, the prattle I brushed aside as humdrum or picayune had a truly Shakespearean majesty and sweep; collected on celluloid, it might wring the withers of moviegoers across the nation, send them alternately sobbing and chuckling into a thousand lobbies to extol my genius. I saw myself fêted as the poet of the mundane, the man who had probed beneath the banality and commonplaceness of the American home and laid bare its essential nobility. The thought of the prestige and money about to accrue made me so giddy that I felt a need to lie down, but as I was already lying down I merely removed the *Times* from my face and consolidated my plans. Using the family as actors, and the Rossellini method of improvisation, I would make a documentary of an afternoon in the life of some average New York apartment dwellers. I summoned my kin and excitedly outlined the project. My wife's enthusiasm was immediate, though she cloaked it under a show of apathy; it was evident she was livid at not having conceived the idea herself.

"A really crackpot notion," she admitted, confusing the word with "crackerjack" with typical feminine disregard for the niceties of slang. "You've outdone yourself this time."

"I ought to be the star," whined my son, an eleven-year-old house urchin. "I was in our school play last year."

"No, me, me!" shrilled his sister. "I want to wear Mummy's mascara!"

"Get this, Mr. Burbage," I snapped, "and you too, Dame Terry.

This is one picture without stars, or makeup, or any of that Hollywood muck. I want authenticity, see? Don't try to act; just be natural. Behave as if there were no camera there at all."

"If you want *complete* realism," began my wife, her face brightening hopefully, "why not do away with the cam —"

"That'll do," I interposed. "Now put on your *rebozos* and slope out of here, the lot of you. I've got a pretty heavy production schedule, and I haven't time to *schmoos* with actors. Remember, everybody on the set tomorrow at three sharp — we start grinding whether you're here or not." I spent the remainder of the day as a seasoned old showman would, gulping bicarbonate of soda, reading *Variety,* and evolving a trademark for my stationery. The trademark offered something of a problem. After toying with the idea of combining the emblems of J. Arthur Rank and M-G-M, to show a slave striking a lion, I rejected it as Socialistic and devised one that portrayed a three-toed sloth pendant from a branch, over the motto "Multum in Parvo." The exhibitors might not understand it too well, and, frankly, I didn't either, but it had dignity and a nice swing to it.

The first player to report at the appointed hour next day was my son; he entered the foyer wearing an Indian war bonnet and a bathrobe, an outfit that did not seem characteristic of a lad fresh from school, especially in the dead of winter. He assured me, though, that he and his mates occasionally liked to vary their standard costume of snow jackets and arctics, and I got a trucking shot of a small Indian in a pitch-black hallway that I will match against anything of the sort Hollywood has to offer. Renewing my strictures that my son was to behave spontaneously and follow his normal routine, I dissolved to the living room, crouched down between the andirons, and prepared to take an arresting camera angle of his movements, shooting through the fire screen. In a rather self-conscious, stagy manner, the boy deposited his briefcase on a table, lit a pipe, and, settling into an armchair, buried himself in an article on Kierkegaard in the *Antioch Review.*

"Hold on a second, Buster," I said, puzzled. "There's something wrong here. I don't know what it is, but an artificial note's crept in. Somehow I get the feeling you're acting. Think hard — is this what you actually do every afternoon?"

"Sure." He nodded. "Sometimes I add up the checkbook and then kick the dog, the way you do. Shall I do that?" Eventually, I managed to impress on him the difference between reality and make-believe, a distinction philosophers have been struggling to clarify for the last twelve hundred years, and he consented to re-enact his habitual procedure, warning me, in all fairness, that it might entail a certain amount of damage.

"Smash anything you like," I ordered impatiently. "Let's have the truth, the more gusto the better. The rest is mere bookkeeping." He shrugged and, retrieving his briefcase, scaled it across the room to indicate how he generally discarded it. An exquisite porcelain Buddha that had cost me thirty dollars and two days of haggling in Hong Kong crashed to the floor. It made such a superb closeup that I could not repress a cry of elation.

"Bravo! Tiptop!" I encouraged. "Whatever you do, keep rolling — don't break the rhythm! I'm getting it all!" Humming a gay little air, the actor turned into the kitchen and helped himself to a bowl of rice pudding, half a cream cheese, an orange, a stalk of celery, and a glass of charged water, leaving the cap off the bottle and the door of the refrigerator open. I then panned with him to the breadbox, where he surreptitiously trailed his finger through the icing on a chocolate cake and nibbled the corner of a napoleon. In the ensuing shot, another transition, we milked the hall closet for some surefire footage. He made a routine check of my overcoat, observing that he frequently found change in the pockets and that it tended to gather rust if left there indefinitely. On the threshold of his room, a strange hesitancy overcame him. He paused, obviously loath to reveal the next phase for fear of parental censure.

"I — I just turn on Jack Armstrong and do my homework till it's time to black Sister's eye," he said evasively.

"Come, come," I prodded. "We're not in the cutting room yet. You left something out."

"Well-l-l," he said, "once in a while I blow up the toilet."

"What for?" I demanded, aghast.

"Nothing," he replied. "It makes a nice sound." All the fellas, it appeared on cross-examination, diverted themselves with this scholarly pastime, and since I realized that my canvas must stand or fall on its fidelity to nature, I set myself to film it. Preparations were soon complete; with smooth efficiency, the boy emptied a can of lye into the bowl, attached a long cord to the handle, and, flinging a lighted match into the lye, yanked the cord. There was a moment's ominous silence. Then a roar like the bombardment of Port Arthur shook the plumbing, and a nine-foot geyser of water reared skyward, subsiding in a curtain of mist. The effect, photographically speaking, was similar to what one sees when standing under Niagara Falls (except for the towels and the toothbrushes in the background, of course); actuarially speaking, it shortened my life ten years. The end result, nevertheless, was worth while, for in his exultation the child uttered a line immeasurably more graphic than that of Rossellini's young hero.

"My goodness!" he exclaimed. "I'd certainly hate to have to mop up all that water!"

"Don't cut, don't cut!" I shouted. "Leave it in!" The fact that we had no sound equipment and that Junior's *mot* had not been recorded in the first place weakened my position somewhat, but then, you can't have everything.

With the poor sense of timing you might expect of amateurs, my wife and daughter chose this, of all moments, to arrange their entrance, arms heaped with groceries, and in the restricted area of the foyer I was unable to jockey the camera to obtain a first-rate composition. The good woman instantly raised a hue and cry over the state of the bathroom, forgetful of the fundamental movie axiom that omelets are never made without breaking eggs. My brief statement that we had simply blown up the toilet reassured her, however, and, **19**

Then a roar like the bombardment of Port Arthur shook the plumbing . . .

pointing out how the overhead was piling up, I urged her to go about her customary activities. A sequence chock-full of human interest resulted, in which she deliberately mislaid or hid all my important papers and shirt studs, sent out the wrong ties to the cleaners, and made a series of dinner dates on the telephone with people she knew I could not abide. To quicken the tempo and ensure flexibility of mood, I intercut several shots of my daughter daubing water colors on the rug and writhing in a tantrum before her music stand.

"Capital," I applauded my troupe. (Performers, and very young ones in particular, are like children — you have to play upon their vanity.) "Now, son," I said, "you'll have to handle the camera, because here's where I usually come home." To a man, they all cringed involuntarily, but my directorial eye was quick to detect and rectify the fallacy. "Get those two shakers of Martinis ready, and remember, everyone, shouts of glee when Daddy walks in." In a trice, I had slipped into the part — merely a matter of sagging a shoulder or two and assuming a murderous scowl. Just as I was shuffling toward the outside door to build up suspense for my arrival, it burst open violently, and three characters I had not foreseen in my budget catapulted in. In the order of their ascending hysteria, they were the furnaceman, the elevator boy, and the superintendent. The last carried what we theatrical folk call a prop — a fire ax — and, in the parlance of the greenroom, he was winging.

The scene that followed, though noisy and fraught with tension, was of little cinematic consequence. It dealt with some argle-bargle about a flood in the apartment below, and its audience appeal, except to plumbers and, possibly, a lawyer or two, would be slight. I understand that additional scenes, or "retakes," are to be made on it very shortly in Essex Market Court. I may drop down there just out of sheer curiosity. My schedule isn't nearly as heavy as it was, now that I've shut down active production at the studio.

Danger in the Drain

CASE HISTORIES from Macy's Bureau of Standards' files. THE CASE OF THE INDELIBLE BATH. *Offered to Macy's:* a preparation purported to reduce obese persons while bathing. *Rejected* for its dubious merits, with the side comment that should a few drops of iodine chance to fall into the tub while this preparation was being used, the bather would turn a bright and unforeseen blue. In drugs, you are protected by city, state, and federal authorities. In Macy's, you are further protected by our own tests, run off on the spot, when we consider stocking anything. —*Macy adv. in the Times.*

INSPECTOR GREGORY STAINES, second in command of the Central Confidential Division of Macy's Bureau of Standards (frivolously referred to as C.C.D.M.B.S. by those "in the know" if they deem one trustworthy and unlikely to tattle), leaned his elbows on the checked tablecloth of our booth in the Blue Ribbon and regarded me quizzically out of a mild blue eye. It was the only one he could regard me out of, the other having atrophied permanently over the years from excessive waggishness. A large, shaggy sheep dog of a man, Gregory affects a deliberate untidiness in his dress and constantly pulls on a foul-smelling pipe, in accord with the prevailing convention in detectives. Though the pipe causes him acute nausea and he is constitutionally thin and meticulous, an unremitting study of English crime films and the novels of Georges Simenon has helped make him authentic. It has required a perseverance and gluttony few men are capable of to transform himself into a picturesque slob, but Staines has done it. As for his ability, that is unquestioned. There is no eye quicker to spy a defective bit of kapok in a mattress, nobody who can sniff out with such celerity the single mildewed olive in the jar. Not for nothing — in other words, for something — do his admiring co-workers call him the Bulldog of the Bureau.

"I say, old man," he observed tolerantly. "Of course, it's none of my business, but aren't you playing rather fast and loose with your dry cleaner?"

"Why, how do you mean?" I asked, nonplussed. Gregory has a way of pouncing when one is sodden with cheesecake that makes it easy to understand why his colleagues also call him the Jaguar of the Bureau.

"Your sleeve," he pointed out. "It's resting in a pool of ketchup." I looked down with a surprised start. It was true; his uncanny orb, swift to note minutiae the layman overlooks, had unerringly spotted the deviation from the norm. As I hastened, somewhat flustered, to sponge it off, Gregory revealed how he had arrived at his conclusion. "I thought at first it was blood," he disclosed, "but then I saw an upset condiment bottle next to it, and ruled out all possibilities until I hit on the right one."

"It sounds easy enough when you explain it," I said ruefully.

"Just routine." He shrugged. "By the way, better brush those caraway seeds off your vest while you're at it. We've found down at the Bureau that the spores work their way into tweed and produce a condition in the wearer known as 'dismay.'" He went on to relate an instance where poppy seeds that had become embedded in a customer's suit in a West Side delicatessen had led to a bothersome action for damages against Macy. The customer, alleging that he was continually being beset by flocks of English sparrows, charged that the seeds had originally been woven into the fabric. Weeks of patient investigation, costly chemical analyses, and the testimony of scores of witnesses had been needed to refute his claim.

"Extraordinary life you chaps lead," I commented. "Take that case

Submitting
merchandise
to normal
wear.

of yours I read about in the *Times* — the reducing preparation that turned its users bright blue."

"The *Times?*" He frowned. "What's that?" For a man whose knowledge is practically encyclopedic, Staines at times betrays a surprising ignorance of his environment. I told him it was a daily newspaper serving the New York area.

"I don't believe I know it," he ruminated. "At any rate, that *was* a puzzler, the affair of the indelible bath. Care to hear the story?"

"No," I replied. Gregory knocked the ashes from his pipe into the sugar bowl, stirred the mixture reflectively, and began. It was as strange a tale, God wot, as those hoary walls had heard in many a moon, and when he got through telling it, they were no younger.

The first inkling Staines had that anything was amiss was the arrival, on a raw March morning, as he was finishing a kipper in his office, of a messenger with a chit from Grimsditch, his superior. Not to put too fine a point on it, Gregory was feeling a bit peckish. To begin with, he abhors kippers and forces himself to eat them only because it is unthinkable for an inspector to start the day otherwise. For another thing, Grimsditch's chits — or the chits of Grimsditch, to employ a more felicitous phrase — are totally unnecessary. His office is right next door, and he could as easily have summoned Gregory over the ground-glass partition. But his colonial love of ceremony (he trained in various remote outposts like Neiman-Marcus in Dallas and Gump's in San Francisco) finds its outlet in these irritating formalities. With a sigh, Gregory detached the gas ring he had used to broil the fish and stowed it in his desk. Under his breath, he cursed the regulations that forbade Macy employees to cook during store hours, forcing them into a hundred ignoble stratagems. For, you see, Gregory is something of an idealist *manqué*.

"Humph," growled Grimsditch when his subordinate entered. "Morning, Staines. I'd appreciate a moment or two of your valuable time, if I'm not interrupting an after-breakfast nap." Gregory was not sure, but he thought he detected an undercurrent of sarcasm in the

Old Man's greeting. More than likely, he had got the wind up over some customer's complaint, and so it proved.

"Look at that!" he snapped, extending a half-eaten baby rattle. "Woman from Sunnyside brought it in this morning. Our guarantee says it's inedible."

"Our guarantee *is* inedible," retorted Staines. "I defy anybody —"

"No, no, man, the *rattle*," Grimsditch broke in, exasperated. "I thought our laboratory had tested it."

"They did," said Gregory. "I had two of the junior operatives teething on it for donkey's years." He scrutinized the toy closely and straightened up in triumph. "No baby chewed that," he declared positively. "Those are the tooth marks of a three-year-old schnauzer."

"The deuce you say!" exclaimed Grimsditch.

"Unmistakable," Gregory said. "Note the aggressive upward sweep of the canines, the powerful, even crunch of the molars. You are familiar with my monograph on the tooth marks of the three-year-old schnauzer?"

"No, but I certainly plan to be," said Grimsditch, impressed. "By gad, my boy, I shan't forget the way you handled this."

"Nothing at all, sir." Gregory dismissed it. "I merely used the old think-box, is all. What's new in that matter of the reducing preparation?"

"Blowed if I know," confessed the chief peevishly. "We can't break down the manufacturer's claim that it melts away the fat — three of our researchers disappeared completely yesterday — but it also seems to affect the pigmentation. Here's the chart." Gregory's forehead puckered as his eye skimmed over the findings; something was definitely out of whack. Latrobe and Shenstone had turned forest green as a result of bathing in the solution, Kugler had emerged streaked with vermilion, and Dismukes was a rich cocoa-brown plaid. Furthermore, the colors were fast; pumice, paint remover, and even emery wheels had been tried without success on the subjects' skins.

"Mind if I take a dekko at the experiment?" proposed Staines. Deep in his subconscious, a hypothesis, as yet little more than intuitive, **27** was forming that some unknown element in the bath must be responsible for the change. Grimsditch, helpless in the face of an enigma that had baffled the keenest minds in the department, embraced the offer eagerly. Placing his entire resources at Gregory's disposal, he escorted him to the door and slipped a compact blue-nickeled charge account into his palm.

"I don't think you'll need it," he counseled, "but if any agents from Saks-Thirty-fourth Street or Altman's are mixed up in this, it's just as well to be prepared." Gregory thanked him and, descending to the kitchenwares, in the basement, took an elevator to the testing laboratory on the roof. To anyone watching him, the maneuver might have appeared purposeless; years of experience, however, had taught him the value of extreme caution. He made his way through a sunny workroom in which besmocked technicians were engaged in tasting oilcloth, setting fire to girdles, jumping up and down on bedsprings, and generally submitting merchandise to normal wear. One of the more unusual probes going forward involved a wheel to each of whose spokes was affixed a metal foot; in the five years the wheel had been revolving, the feet were estimated to have covered a distance of six hundred thousand miles. Inasmuch as Macy's did not sell metal feet, the object of the inquiry was not too clear, but, thought Gregory, it made a whiz-bang display.

Crabtree, the head supervisory engineer, was awaiting him when he reached the drug section; Grimsditch had sent ahead a chit to herald Gregory's advent. Crabtree was answerable only to Grimsditch, and Grimsditch, in turn, was answerable only to Crabtree — an arrangement that ensured a maximum of harmony and prevented leaks. The strain of the past couple of days had begun to tell on the engineer. His usually rubicund physiognomy was ashen and his face had paled perceptibly.

"Frankly, we're up a tree," Crabtree admitted, conducting Staines into an improvised bathroom where a fat man was disrobing. "We're convinced some foreign substance is tinting our guinea pigs, but hanged if we can isolate the blamed thing. Are you ready, Wagenhals?" The fat man returned a melancholy nod and lowered himself gingerly into the steaming bath. Crabtree, about to add the obesity fluid, suddenly checked his hand.

"What's the matter?" he inquired of the man. "Don't you feel well?"

"I'm O.K.," croaked Wagenhals, his expression belying his words. "It's only — well, I — I heard a rumor that folks looked different after bathing in here."

"Different in what way?"

"That — that they turned various colors, like purple, and orange —"

"Now, hold on, Wagenhals," said Crabtree impatiently. "Have you ever seen any orange people?"

"Just in *Lassie*," faltered the man, "and one time I saw a whaling picture with Don Ameche —"

"Exactly," interposed Crabtree. "Well, forget that cafeteria gossip. You know how people love to talk." He emptied the solvent into the water; instantaneously its surface boiled into an agitated froth, lashing the sides of the tub with extraordinary violence. Had Gregory been watching the bather, he might have seen a hint of clavicle appear below the fleshy throat, the double chin grow taut, but his eyes were pinned on the medicine chest in the wall above Wagenhals' head. Its door was 'ajar, and from an overturned bottle inside, bluish drops splashed into the bath below.

"Look, look!" cried Crabtree. "He's turning indigo!"

Staines paid him no heed. With the peculiar, catlike spring that earned him the sobriquet of the Polecat of the Bureau, he crossed the floor in a single bound, caught up the bottle, and slammed shut the door of the cabinet. "Get this man into a tubful of fresh water at once!" he barked at the amazed Crabtree. "Another sixty seconds in that witch's broth and I won't answer for the consequences."

"But I don't understand," quavered Crabtree. "What was in the bottle?"

"Eyewash," said Gregory sternly. "An ordinarily innocuous liquid that, as we have learned to our considerable chagrin, can play strange chemical pranks on the unwary, and that, along with iodine, **29** hair tonic, after-shave lotion, and a host of other brews, you have thoughtlessly allowed to fall into the testing medium." And, leaving an open-mouthed Crabtree to fold a considerably diminished Wagenhals into a pretested towel, he went downstairs to file his report.

"Well, there you have it," concluded Staines, refilling the bowl of his pipe with ashes and sugar. "The clue was right under their noses, but, of course, they hadn't the sense to see it. Pure, unadulterated eyewash, found in every bathroom."

"Not to mention one other place," I suggested diffidently.

"What's that?"

"Advertising copy," I said.

Staines rose majestically. "I consider that remark in very poor taste," he announced, "and I intend to convey it to Grimsditch at once." Before I could temporize, he had jammed on his hat and stalked from the restaurant. Not until three seconds after he had gone did I realize that he had forgotten to pay the check. For a man whose love of detail has made his name a watchword at the Blue Ribbon, Staines is at times surprisingly lax.

Little Boy Grue

THE LAST TIME I had my fortune told, at a tearoom that furnishes me with amazingly reliable knowledge of the future, I do not recall the gypsy astrologer's making any mention of a big-game huntress in my horoscope. The sibyl accurately prophesied the proximity of a tall, dark man (the overdraft clerk at my bank); she sensed cloth smoldering (I burned a hole in my best flannel slacks during the séance, and they had to be artistically rewoven at prohibitive cost); and she saw a house of cards collapsing (an uncanny portent of the fate in store for my operetta about Coxey's Army, which a producer was weighing at the moment). Nowhere, however, was there any intimation that I would be preoccupied presently with a fair Nimrod, and a twelve-year-old one at that. The augury spoke of a sharpshooter's hovering near me, but I naturally took it to mean the producer. I never dreamed it might refer to a Midwestern schoolgirl who is currently stalking the Congo around Lake Albert and giving those wart hogs, to say nothing of the deponent, a lively case of chills and fever.

Let me say at the outset that I have still to meet this gifted child, whose name is Elaine Monesmith and who hails from Dayton, Ohio; all I know of her is what I gleaned from a recent story in the *Mirror*, printed shortly after she had left on her second expedition into Africa. On her first, a year ago, Elaine's marksmanship was already so unerring that she bagged a lion, three Cape buffaloes, an antelope, and a sizable quantity of smaller game. She also displayed a poise you would normally associate with such seasoned sportsmen as Paul Du Chaillu and Carl Akeley. Said her father, describing an incident when a wounded buffalo charged their guide, a native, and himself, "It was a terribly close shave. We ran desperately, frantically, trying to escape after each of us were able to fire one shot. But it was a single bullet from Elaine's rifle that brought down the beast and saved our lives. She had been watching the hunt from a hill above the swamp." Truly an exploit not to be sneezed at, even making allowances for an obviously doting parent. Hitherto, continues the *Mirror's* account, Elaine's arsenal has consisted of a .35-caliber Remington, a .32-caliber automatic pistol, and a hunting knife; on the present safari she will also use a .375 Winchester Magnum, as she hopes to pot an elephant and a rhinoceros. To demonstrate her essential stability, though, and pursuant to the axiom that every prodigy, whether chess wizard or mathematician, is, *au fond*, a healthy, mischievous youngster, the article adds quickly, "An eighth-grade student, she plays the trumpet in the school band and plans to be a surgeon when she grows up. Meanwhile, she intends to keep a day-by-day diary of her adventures and will write a book when she returns."

It requires no particular editorial flair to detect in that last sentence one of the hottest publishing ideas in a decade. Considering the avidity with which the public has strained to its bosom the reminiscences of far less colorful characters, like taxi-drivers and sandhogs, Elaine's African memoirs are bound to be a natural. The hair-raising thrills she experiences, set down with unaffected juvenile candor, must unquestionably result in a best-seller. Whether it will distill the full flavor of her complex personality, it is, of course, impossible to gauge in advance. Nevertheless, it is interesting to conjecture the nature of a journal kept by an exceptional moppet exposed to the perils of the Dark Continent. Just as a makeshift until Elaine releases hers, and as a sort of preview, I offer one compiled, under similar circumstances, by an equally talented eleven-year-old of my acquaintance. His name is Rusty Kipness and he was at one time a classmate of my son, through whose kind intercession I am enabled to quote portions of it. Here and there, where the diarist's erudition has led him to lapse into Greek and Sanskrit, I have taken the liberty of translating for clarity's sake.

S.S. AFRIKAANDER BELLE, JUNE 4
LAT. 4° S. LONG. 40° E.

La Rochefoucauld was right; if you don't do a thing yourself, it'll never get done. I told the captain of this old tub the other night that the ship was off its course, but he just brushed me off. "A fat lot you know about it, wise guy," he said. "I'm the master of this vessel and I tell you we'll be in Mombasa in three days. Now run along and oil your Mannlicher." That's the thanks you get for trying to help people out. "O.K., Captain Kuyp," I said to him. "You watch. You keep on this way and you'll end up on the East African coastal shelf." Sure enough, the middle of last night there was a pounding on the door of the cabin I share with my father. I jumped up, every faculty at the ready, and wrenched open the door. The Captain, whimpering and wringing his hands, was standing just outside in the passageway, tears running down his sextant. "Rusty! Rusty, what'll I do?" he was sobbing. "The keel is practically plowing a furrow through the center of Zanzibar! I should have heeded the counsel of younger and wiser heads." Well, I went up on the bridge and had them throw the wheel hard over, which any ten-year-old idiot could see was indicated, and pretty soon everything was in apple-pie order. Of course, the minute the danger was past, I was a brat again. It was "Don't touch the whistle" and "Get the hell out of the chartroom," as if they'd never set eyes on me before. That's what I like about grownups: Do them a favor and they'll give you the shirt off their back — right in your face.

But maybe I'm getting ahead of my story and should introduce myself. Nobody's ever going to see these pages but me and possibly half a dozen publishers; still, there's no percentage in pretending to be a trey of spades when you're really a face card. I guess the name of Rusty Kipness is synonymous with God wherever folks use firearms. I can shoot anything that flies, slinks, creeps, or crawls, at any range, standing, sitting, blindfolded, asleep, awake, or with both hands tied behind me. My scrapbooks, cups, trophies, medals, and ribbons take up two floors in the Manhattan Storage Warehouse; I've won every major trapshooting competition in the world since I was five; and the New York Police Department pays me fifteen thousand a year as its unofficial adviser on ballistics. Yet underneath my grave exterior there lurks an unspoiled, high-spirited American boy. When I can steal time from the Institute for Advanced Studies at Princeton, where I occasionally lend a hand to Dr. Einstein, I like to bury myself in my stamp collection. I play the traps indifferently (Gene Krupa is much better, though he denies it), my billiards are a cut below Willie Hoppe's, and I dabble in sculpture, now and then executing a trifle mistaken for the work of Maillol. I haven't settled on my future profession definitely, but if you drop a line to the White House after 1960, I think it'll reach me without any trouble.

Well, that about covers the ground, except to add that I got embroiled in this expedition only as a gesture to (of all things) a café proprietor. I was at El Morocco a couple of months ago and John Perona began badgering me for some fresh zebra skins to upholster his banquettes. I could have fobbed off fake ones just as easily, but, big-hearted slob that I am, I had to promise him the real McCoy. My old man threw a tantrum at first — said it was quixotic and prodigal — and I suppose it was. Anyway, I softened him up by letting him pose with me for the newsreels before we sailed, and now he's as excited as a kid. You have to know how to get around grownups. Talk about your egomaniacs; if I ever have a son, I certainly won't bring him up to be an adult.

NAIROBI, JUNE 14

It sure will be a relief to quit this hornets' nest; I haven't drawn a quiet breath since we checked in, a week ago. Parades, dinners, garden parties — you'd think they'd never seen a genius before. The whole town's plastered with bunting and streamers reading "Welcome, Rusty Kipness," and I can't put my nose out of the hotel without autograph-seekers' closing in like a cloud of locusts. The officials are even worse. I don't know how they solved their problems heretofore, but now, whenever a crisis looms, I'm the patsy. Day before yesterday, one of the carp in the fountains at Government House took a crazy notion, the way carp do, and went berserk. It leaped out of the pool into a hogshead standing near by and started thrashing around, hurling the secretarial staff into a panic. They ran into the legislature, where I was straightening out the members on the Swahili question, and begged me to take over. I emptied a couple of slugs into the cask; nothing, really — it was as easy as shooting fish in a barrel — but I can still hear the hosannas ringing in my ears. The same way Friday, when they rushed me to the hospital to remove a tick from the Colonial Secretary. I'm not actually a medical man, although I know the rudiments and I've invented a suture or two that have revolutionized surgery. Well, you never saw such a commotion. After the operation, the nurses formed on the lawn and spelled out, "Rusty Kipness has breathed new life into the Hippocratic oath, emblazoning his name beside those of Harvey, Jenner, Semmelweiss, and Sir William Osler" (they have a lot of nurses in the Nairobi hospital), and the internes carried me on their shoulders to the city limits. Frankly, it was a bit on the fulsome side.

Tomorrow, we pull out for the bush. I believe the change of scene will do my old man good. Of late, he has been quite snappish; every time I give him a word of friendly advice, he flies into a pet. Today, while he was shaving, I borrowed the razor and explained how to get maximum efficiency from each stroke. His neck turned a peculiar violet color, and he beat his fists on the basin and screamed some phrase I couldn't catch about the last straw. Physically, Pop is beginning to show his years. Mentally, he is still as spry as a baby.

NGOROGORO CRATER, JUNE 29

We have been camped here about a fortnight, and, for all the action I've seen, I might as well be on a quilting bee. Half a dozen moth-

. . . *you could doze on your porch at Far Rockaway and pick off better game.*

eaten lions, a small herd of giraffes, and thirty or forty miserable little elands, hartbeests, and gnus — you could doze on your porch at Far Rockaway and pick off better game. If I could only miss a few, at least there'd be an element of chance, but I can't trick my reflexes; once I get the quarry in my sights, it's doomed. The trouble with being infallible is that it creates a gulf between you and your fellows. The beaters and gunbearers have some absurd notion in their pates that I'm superhuman; they don't even bother to run out and see whether I've made a kill, because it's a foregone conclusion. Todhunter, our guide (the old man insisted we take one along, though I know the terrain inside out), is so consumed with envy that he won't leave his tent. Lord knows I've met him halfway, given him repeated pointers on collecting spoors for pleasure and profit and pacifying a rogue elephant, but the man is clearly a tyro — strictly out of this veldt.

Shipped off those zebra pelts to Perona yesterday, and, brother, am I glad *that* headache is over! What a chore, finding specimens of exactly the right size to fit his benches; if I weren't such a meatball, I'd bill him for my time and ammunition. I hope Dan Topping and Serge Obolensky and that crowd appreciate what I've gone through in their behalf. Probably not. More than likely, they'll sit back on their fat banquettes and take it all for granted.

The old gent is in a vile mood; he's turned into a regular crosspatch. Last night, for a gag, I sneaked into his tent and gave him a bat foot; that is, I draped a vampire bat over his toe, which was sticking out of the mosquito bar. It couldn't have hurt him, needless to say, on account of I extracted the fangs; just tickled a little. Well, in about five minutes he let out a holler they must have heard in Bloemfontein. Instead of behaving rationally and going back to sleep, he tore down the tent and rolled around in the canvas, screaming himself blue. After he calmed down, I told him it was a rib, and then the fireworks started. I can stand being whaled with a cartridge belt, but he should have realized I'd lose face with that circle of grinning Kaffirs looking on. Something's changed him; we're not the buddies we used to be.

UJIJI, TANGANYIKA, JULY 20

My premonition was right; the situation vis-à-vis the pater finally blew up with a bang ten days ago and I had to walk out on him. There's no living with a bird who can't take a joke; if he'd only looked at the viper in his cot, he could have seen it was an old snakeskin stuffed with cotton, and not a mamba. Anyhow, I was good and fed up by the time he finished working over me, so I just threw some things in a bag and hit the road. It's a longish trek across the Belgian Congo to Brazzaville — about eleven hundred miles, and largely wooded — but I'm in pretty fair condition and I don't expect to let any grass grow under my feet. This is where Stanley found Livingstone, by the way — quite a historic spot, in view of the fact that I'm beginning my hike through the Congo from here, too. The authorities have been plaguing me to dedicate a tablet to that effect. As if that's all I have on my mind — dedicating tablets for authorities. Good grief, can't they ever let a person alone?

CAPETOWN, SEPTEMBER 2

Well, the old man has the laugh on me and I'm sport enough to admit it; I guess I don't know my Africa, after all. I must have got turned around or something — in my foolish pride it never occurred to me to ask directions — for, first thing I noticed, I'd passed Victoria Falls, traversed Bechuanaland, and was up to my hips in Boers. It was too late to slip into town incognito; they spotted me the second I entered the suburbs. The whole Union of South Africa's in a lather, and apparently I'm the biggest news since the Kohinoor diamond. Flags, speeches, receptions, and the usual nightmare — it's all I can do to hang on to my sense of proportion. Ah, well, the fat's in the fire and I may as well make the best of it. I've had a nice ramble and a summer in the open air, I'm persona grata with Perona, and I won't have to be tutored in geography. That always was my Achilles' heel. **39**

Monet Makes the World Go Round

A B O U T a month ago, a very nice married pair I know, whose life had been moderately placid and devoid of heartache up to that point, was unexpectedly overtaken by calamity. Without any warning, a play of theirs on Broadway was snapped up by the movies, they themselves were hired to destroy it at a weekly stipend running into four income-tax blanks, and they were ordered to report in Hollywood inside a fortnight. The suddenness of the blow, coming out of a clear sky, might well have unseated the couple's reason, but their friends loyally rallied to their aid and, summoning all the tact and sympathy they could muster, tried to palliate the harshness of their plight. I was one of several who, on the eve of their leave-taking, called to condole and wish them Godspeed, and I was hard put to think of a suitable going-away present. A gift of money or books did not seem appropriate; they had enough of the former to stave off acute want, and as for literature, their reading days were over. I wanted something that not only would typify the land they were going to but would reconcile them to it, a memento, if possible, that would ease the burden of southern California when it grew intolerable. It was a tall order, but I finally filled it. You might think the token I gave them, the business card of a real-estate agent, was prosaic. And yet the party it introduced them to and described may easily be the greatest man who ever lived.

I have never met Realtor N. Rodes, I regret to say; I found his card thrust under the windshield wiper of my rented Scripps-Booth phaeton the last time I quit the Vine Street Brown Derby. One side of the card, celebrating a local realty-and-loan company and its manifold facilities for insurance, management, and investment, bore the injunction "Ask Realtor N. Rodes." The stature of the man became apparent from the text on the reverse:

Realtor Rodes is a man who goes through life helping, serving, building up, encouraging, cheering, stimulating, assuring, comforting, radiating love, which is the greatest constructive force in the Universe. Realtor Rodes never knocks, he always declares the Truth, and if there be any error present, it fades away, as error must always fade in the presence of Truth. People respect Realtor Rodes and are always happy to see him. Realtor Rodes makes life a little easier, makes the rough road a little smoother, makes service a joy, makes sorrow less heavy to bear, makes love take the place of hate, success the place of failure, health the place of sickness and disease. . . . Realtor Rodes is very patient, very kind, knows no jealousy, makes no parade, gives himself no airs, is never rude, never selfish, never irritated, never resentful, never glad when others go wrong, always slow to expose, always eager to believe the best, always hopeful and cheerful.

Had I had the time and a first mortgage, I would have considered it a rare privilege to sit down and negotiate a second one with a person combining the attributes of Gautama Buddha, Clara Barton, Father Zossima, and Little Nell. Unfortunately, I was overdue in Playa del Rey, where I had promised to contract a case of botulism from eating a poisoned avocado salad at the home of an acquaintance, and I left the Pacific Slope without ever seeing Mr. Rodes. This morning, strangely, I again caught myself thinking of him, and California real-estate dealers in general, after I read an advertisement in a magazine called *What's Doing*, published at Monterey in the Golden State.

"Studio Home for sale," it ran, "on Huckleberry Hill, New Monterey Artist Colony. Modern artist preferred, post-Impressionist acceptable. If writer, must bring sample of work and pay full cash. $5,500; down payment, $2,500. Preble & Nickele, 252 Lighthouse Avenue."

The forthrightness of the wording, the simple, uncomplicated summation of an ideal, wrung an involuntary grunt of approval from me. There was no ambiguity, no jiggery-pokery about the matter; the agents did not want any pre-Raphaelite or fusty academician lousing up the premises, and if tragic necessity forced them to accept a writer, they at least asked a precautionary hinge at his adverbs and a resilient financial cushion, whether he be Thomas Mann or avant-garde poet. Nevertheless, it struck me that such inflexible conditions must impose a strain on the average artist. His antipathy to the businessman is sometimes acute, and to have to truckle to the latter's aesthetic standards or be denied shelter is a harrowing choice. I suggest that advertisements of this nature could lead to a variety of singular situations, one of which I append to show what I mean. (It should always be remembered, of course, that I frequently don't know what I mean.)

The office of Gouge & Flint, Realtors, was a modest, whitewashed bungalow with a red tile roof, sandwiched in between a souvenir shop full of Mexican handicrafts and pottery bookends and an anemic lending library that mailed stuffed dates to any part of the world, post-free. As Simeon and Drusilla Quagmeyer drove toward it down a weedy back street of Monterey and saw the cars clustered along the curb, Drusilla uttered a vengeful snort.

"I told you we should have started earlier," she said. "They probably sold the place hours ago." She was a thin, intense girl with a black bang, fretful and somewhat inclined to nag her slow-moving, phlegmatic husband.

"Now, take it easy," advised Simeon. "The ad only came out yesterday, and there aren't so many post-Impressionists around with twenty-five hundred dollars."

"Well, if you *like* painting in two rooms over a garage in Carmel," Drusilla snapped, "if you *enjoy* seeing me write a historical novel behind a beaverboard partition . . ."

"Plenty of housewives write them in their kitchens, with six kids hanging to their apron strings," observed Simeon. "I read it in the women's magazines all the time."

"Yes, and they sound like it," Drusilla bristled. "Well, I'm glad to know what you really think of *Spoon Bread and Powder Horns.*" She lapsed into a sulky silence.

Simeon finished backing the car into a vacant space and shut off the ignition. "Come on, puss," he said, patting his wife's shoulder placatingly. "Haven't I said from the beginning your book is the best thing since *The Manatee*? I need this studio as much as you do — if I can only pass the exam."

Mollified, Drusilla descended and stood waiting while Simeon withdrew a canvas from the rumble seat. "Which one are you submitting?" she asked anxiously. " 'Fish-Net Fugue, Pebble Beach'?"

"No, 'Sea Wrack with Raisins.' It's a shade more abstract."

"Do you think they'll object to the Picasso influence?"

"*What* Picasso influence?" Simeon demanded belligerently. "I had guitars and newspapers in my pictures years before that faker!"

"Of course you did," Drusilla soothed him. "I just wondered how hidebound the judges might be."

"We'll soon find out," said Simeon, turning up the path to the realty office. "Remember, keep mum about your novel or they'll make us cough up full cash."

"You can give me credit for a little sense." She examined her husband critically as he removed his hat. "I wish you hadn't had your hair cut yesterday. It looks terribly conventional."

"I'll rumple it," suggested Simeon. "There, that better?" She nodded and opened the door, almost colliding with a dejected young man also bearing a canvas under his arm. He was being shown out by a portly, florid-faced gentleman in a pepper-and-salt suit.

"Sorry, Kaboolian," the portly man was saying briskly. "Your brushwork's passable, but I'd set fire to the property before I let a primitive live in it. You understand my position, don't you?"

"Oh, sure, sure," mumbled Kaboolian. "It's a question of taste."

"That's right," said the other, smiling, "and you haven't any. Good day." He swung toward the Quagmeyers. "You folks here about that studio? Have a seat. We'll interview you after we take care of these fellows." He beckoned to the occupants of the anteroom, two bearded homuncules in berets, and plunged into an inner room. Glancing at Simeon's painting with mingled condescension and triumph, the dwarfs picked up their portfolios and followed the portly man.

"Who were those men?" whispered Drusilla. "I've seen them somewhere."

"The Fulbright brothers," said Simeon. "We met them at the Fig Festival in Tarzana. They do movie paintings."

"What sort?"

"You know, the kind you see on the easel when Alan Ladd is starving in the garret and Herbert Marshall comes to persuade him to return to his wife. Hollow stuff, quite slick."

"Which is which?"

"I'm not sure," said Simeon. "One does foregrounds, the other backgrounds."

"Who puts in the middle?" Drusilla asked.

"Why, Alan Ladd," replied Simeon. "That's what he's doing while Marshall's talking."

From within, there suddenly rang out the sound of voices lifted in altercation.

"That'll do!" they heard an angry full-throated bellow. "There's no room on Huckleberry Hill for anyone who paints beggar boys munching cherries! Out!" Simultaneously, the Fulbrights emerged, scowls contorting their faces, and, escorted by the portly man, were summarily shown the door.

"Philistines," he growled after them. "Ought to be horsewhipped, trying to muscle into a high-grade community with that swill. Well, come in," he commanded the Quagmeyers impatiently. "I haven't got all day."

"My name is Simeon Quag —" began Simeon.

"I don't care if it's Paul Cézanne," the realtor interrupted. "Your picture'll do the talking. And if you're trying to buy that studio, it better be eloquent." He preceded them into a small, severely furnished office. Behind a desk sat a spare, tight-lipped individual in a suit of stiff gray broadcloth, his watch chain strung with fraternal emblems. "This is Flint — I'm Gouge. Stand the canvas on the chair."

"Er — pardon me," put in Drusilla ingratiatingly, "but could you tell us how many rooms the house has? The one we're competing for?"

"Rooms, Madam?" Gouge repeated, as though his ears deceived him. "You have the infernal crust to start discussing *rooms* before we've even passed on your eligibility?"

"*Ought to be horsewhipped, trying to muscle into a high-grade community with that swill.*"

"I — I just wanted to see if it would be suitable for us," Drusilla stammered.

"It's not a case of what's suitable. It's what you rate," rapped out Flint. "Look here, Gouge, if this woman's going to create a disturbance —"

"Please, Drusilla," implored Simeon, wigwagging a frantic entreaty for caution. The realtors dismissed her with a withering stare and subjected the picture to a close scrutiny. Simeon was finding the suspense well-nigh unbearable when Gouge broke it.

"Hmm, not bad," he said grudgingly. "It's derivative — I see Dufy and John Marin written all over it — but you might make a pretty fair tenant if you toned down that cobalt blue a bit."

"His burnt sienna's miserable," grumbled Flint, "and his clouds are right out of a mural in a spaghetti joint."

"Still, it's the best so far," Gouge said, squinting past his thumb at the composition. "Certain amount of vitality, even though there's a complete lack of talent. What do you think?" The partners engaged in a low-pitched deliberation studded with inquisitorial glances at the Quagmeyers. Unconsciously, Drusilla and Simeon drew closer; she could feel his hand trembling in hers as he awaited the verdict.

"You brought the down payment in cash, naturally?" Flint inquired, studying them with cold dispassion.

"Yes, sir, in fives and tens," Simeon assured him eagerly. "They're not all new bills, but I got as many as I could."

"Well," said Gouge reluctantly, "Flint thinks you're a flash in the pan and I daresay he's right. However, we're gamblers. You can have it."

"You mean the whole house, with the roof and everything?" exclaimed Simeon joyfully. "Boy, oh, boy —"

Drusilla, more practical than her spouse, refused to give way to enthusiasm. "I don't suppose there'd be any chance of seeing it before we bought it, would there?" she asked timidly. "A snapshot would do."

"Positively not," retorted Gouge. "We don't do business that way at Gouge & Flint, my good woman. Sight unseen and as is. Now, speak up — do you want the parcel or don't you?"

"Hold on a second," interposed his colleague. "We're overlooking a vital point. What's *your* profession?"

"Me?" Drusilla blinked. Without thinking, she drew herself up proudly. "I write historical novels," she said. Simeon's horrified gasp recalled her promise, and she turned to him in quick contrition. He stood stricken, disillusion with all womankind plain in his eyes.

"I knew it," cackled Flint grimly. "I knew she was a busybody the minute she walked in."

"Well, that alters everything," Gouge frowned. "We can't have people writing indiscriminately all over the place."

"Couldn't you make an exception of her?" begged Simeon, too desperate to weigh his words. "She's a rank tyro, honest. Nobody'll print her —"

"Did she bring along a sample?" queried Flint. His face hardened as Drusilla mutely shook her head. "False pretenses, eh? Thought you'd sneak into the colony posing as a respectable matron."

Stung, Drusilla rummaged in her handbag and whipped out several typescript carbons. "There!" she threw at him defiantly. "Read this love scene if you don't believe me. And here's a letter from Henry Seidel Canby that says it's the most evocative —"

"Yes, yes, baby," Simeon cut in, jockeying her to the door. "You wait in the anteroom. I'll be right out."

"You bet I will," his wife said, glowering. "I've got a few things to take up with you." The door banged violently behind her. Neither Flint nor Gouge, absorbed in the carbons, looked up. The minutes dragged by; in vain Simeon watched the agents for some classifiable response. At last, Flint exhaled a deep sigh and, crumpling the pages into a ball, flung them into a wastebasket. Extracting a handkerchief, he dusted the desk, then drew a deed from his pocket. For the first time, his features betrayed something resembling compassion.

"My boy," he announced soberly, "if that girl's a writer, I'm a ring-tailed monkey. Your wife is a very unfortunate woman."

"I know, I know," Simeon agreed piteously. "But please don't speak so loud. She's probably listening at the keyhole."

"Does she ever beat you?" asked Gouge kindly.

"Not so often," said Simeon. "Once in a while."

"Well," Flint said, rising, "here's the deed, and I wish you luck. Never mind about the money."

"Say," murmured Simeon, overcome. *"Thanks."*

"Forget it," said the realtor brusquely. "When a man paints the way you do and has a wife like that, he needs all the breaks he can get."

The three shook hands wordlessly; Simeon, dazed, moved to the door. He paused with his hand on the knob. "Gosh, what'll I say?" he appealed to them. "How will I ever explain it to her?"

"That's your affair, brother," said Gouge. "God help you, and watch that cobalt blue."

Simeon sucked in a lungful of air and, squaring his shoulders, went out into the anteroom, where Drusilla waited ominously. "Gee, darling," he said, "the darnedest thing happened . . ."

Casanova, Move Over

ON A BALMY morning last month, had you been woolgathering outside Pennsylvania Station, picking your teeth along with a dozen other shepherds engaged in the same pursuit, you might have seen the undersigned alight from a cab and hand down two ladies very like the Langhorne sisters. So marked was the similarity, indeed, that a buzz of admiration, mingled with comments of "What price the Langhorne sisters now?," issued from the bystanders. Long accustomed to the plaudits my wife and her sister arouse, the ovation caused me no particular emotion, other than a fleeting pang that my own startling resemblance to Lord Louis Mountbatten should have passed unnoticed. As the girls strode vivaciously down the arcade, spots of color glowed in their cheeks — partly because they were anticipating the holiday in store for them and partly because they were carrying their own luggage. Every year, when the catkins appear on the willowkins in Schling's, the two shake off their family responsibilities and snatch a blissful weekend at Atlantic City. They sleep until noon, live wholly on brownies and double-cream Alexanders, shop the auction rooms for bargains in bellpulls, and strive to outdo each other with tales of their husbands' maltreatment. This brief catharsis, it is held, restores the stamina necessary to eke out their lives — the best years of which, they hasten to add oracularly, they have expended on a couple of notable tyrants and ingrates.

"Now, what'll you do evenings while I'm away?" my wife asked as I bought her a glassine bag of cashews and a comic for the train.

I replied that I was intending to shellac a paddle I had carved for the children and, in any time that remained, to write a short history of Byzantine art. Her lips tightened in disapproval. "I knew it," she said. "You're going to sit in the house and mope. Why don't you make some dates with people — take a nice girl out to dinner or the theater?" Of course, I pooh-poohed the suggestion as ludicrous and unseemly; for all her concern, I could hardly envision a sober burgess like myself in Bustanoby's or Reisenweber's quaffing champagne wine from a soubrette's slipper. My wife, though, was not so easily deflected. As we exchanged a farewell embrace on the platform, she renewed her appeal. An evening of feminine society, she contended, would enliven a humdrum existence and stimulate me immeasurably. Troubled lest anxiety for my welfare cloud her vacation, I reluctantly agreed to co-operate, and the pair departed blithely for their spree among the carbohydrates.

Naturally, I had no intention whatever of fulfilling the pledge I had airily made, but within no more than five minutes it began to weigh heavy on me. Cursed from boyhood with an exaggerated sense of honor, I gritted my teeth and sought out a barbershop hard by, where I had myself shaved, manicured, shampooed, massaged, and conditioned in general for the fleshpots. Then I consulted my ancient address book, which I had supposed must yield a likely candidate for revelry. Its pages were far from rewarding. The sprightly nurse from Minnesota I had squired about in 1928 was at last reports an affluent *corsetière* in Framingham and the mother of five. Greta, a somnolent blonde off the prow of a Viking ship, as glacial as the diamonds I had showered her with, was chicken-farming on the Rogue River, in Oregon. There had once been a redheaded bobcat named Frankie with a lair on Varick Street, but the encroaching Sixth Avenue subway had flushed her from it, and she had left for parts unknown. The situation, in a word, augured little optimism.

It augured even less after a systematic telephone canvass, in alphabetical order, of the prospects that were left. All the *jeunes 'filles* in my record had either scattered to the four winds or contracted tiresome alliances with some insanely jealous boxer who chained them to the cookstove to prevent their straying. The outlook was becoming bleak indeed when I recalled Chloe, a demure Southern contralto in a musical show I once helped confect. Whether it was desperation or nostalgia for those bygone royalties, I remembered her as exuding a sultry, magnolia-scented charm. Surprisingly enough, she still dwelt at her former address, and her voice came over the wire freighted with the same languor, as though she had just eaten a double serving of spoon bread and yams. Chloe had difficulty identifying me at first, owing to a slight whistling sound produced by my upper plate, but we finally established a rapport and arranged to have cocktails in a chic East Side bar and go on from there to dinner.

Except for two hours spent roaching my hair down to mask its sparsity and trying on a couple of hundred neckties, I made no special preparations for the event. The first impact of Chloe, awaiting me in the anteroom of the bar, was a shade unnerving. The winsome shyness of old had given way to a certain theatrical dash, a definite aura of sophistication. Her shoulder-length hair was a sleek platinum and on it rode a Restoration cavalier's hat of shimmering green velvet the size of a cart wheel. A silver-fox chubby hung open to expose quantities of costume jewelry; her bag, modeled on those carried by postmen, was unaccountably emblazoned with the seal of Rutgers University.

"Sugar!" she caroled, enveloping me in clouds of Carte Blanche, the world's least expensive perfume. "I declare, you've gone and got as plump as a lil biddy shoat!"

I explained that the gray suit I was wearing probably made me look bulkier than I am. "It's a well-known optical illusion," I said. "You know, gray always makes people look heavier. Take me, for instance. Now, actually, I'm a thin person, but every time I put on a gray suit —"

"Listen, honey," she said decisively, "don't try to talk your way out of it. You and June are bustin' out all over. Come on, buy me a drink."

Our entrance into the bar awakened no more comment than would that of a two-headed calf. Of the ten clients dotted around the dim, pine-paneled interior, eight were unknown to me. The remaining two — a gossip columnist and a distant cousin wedded to a lawyer with a flourishing divorce practice, threw me broad, significant winks every time I glanced in their direction. Whatever doubts I had as to the suitability of the rendezvous were quickly banished by Chloe. She adored the sporting prints on the walls, she trilled, and the pink coats of the waiters; they reminded her of an old-time English tavern. "I guess it's because Daddy's Scotch-Irish on his mother's side," she went on with signal irrelevancy. "I get a boot out of those old characters smoking their church-warden pipes and banging the pewter tankards on the table." Several ponies of bourbon, tossed off neat with a dispatch the old characters would have envied, started Chloe's tongue wagging, and she filled me in on her activities. She was not gainfully employed at the moment; Ethel Merman, through nepotism and trickery, had nosed her out of the leading role in *Annie Get Your Gun*. However, if her singing lessons continued at their present gratifying rate, Signor Doloroso predicted that Bidu Sayao would shortly be selling matches. To illustrate, Chloe uncorked an octave of such sheer power that the ashtrays started to dance. Realizing the bar was much too cramped to permit adequate scope for her voice, I tactfully proposed that we adjourn to a small French place whose mussels are the best this side of Saint-Tropez. My vis-à-vis leaped at the idea. She adored mussels; they reminded her of France.

The maître d'hôtel at Chez l'Argent was worldly enough to recognize a man desirous of privacy when he saw one, and, replacing the hors-d'œuvre Chloe had brushed to the floor as we entered the place, he led us to a centrally located table on a spotlighted podium. From this point of vantage, I was able to discern a number of casual acquaintances — friends of my wife more than mine — who interrupted their meal to wave cheerily and jot down memoranda on their cuffs. The profusion of food on the menu enchanted Chloe, who was clearly surfeited with her diet of black-eyed peas and hominy. She ate daintily but unsparingly of foie gras, turtle soup, *truite au bleu,* and pressed duck with oranges, washing them down with a decent 1923 Beaune brought in under escort by a Holmes patrol.

My conversation, while undeniably sparkling, tended to be domestic rather than romantic. The prettiest coquetries I could devise invariably turned into accounts of witticisms the children or the dog had made; at one juncture I caught myself defending with passion a brand of soap powder used in our household. The fault, to be truthful, was not exclusively mine; apart from her parochial absorption in show business, Chloe was impossible to interest. She greeted the wealth of topics I introduced — our new vacuum cleaner, the shoddy quality of slipcovers one purchases nowadays, the butcher's overweening insolence — with an unvarying yawn of fatigue. Pique finally got the better of prudence, and I filed a few strictures on the shallow, frivolous personality typical of denizens of the Gay White Way. The homily had its effect. Drowsily supporting her chin on her hand, she stared deep into my eyes and told me I was cooking with gas.

When it came time to select a fitting liqueur, I learned that our choice of Chez l'Argent that night had been nothing short of providential. The management had just acquired a fabulously rare cognac; needless to say, it was not for sale, but M. Reynard yielded a point and allowed us, as connoisseurs, to inspect the bottle. Thawed by Chloe's soft impeachment, he yielded another point and granted us a thimbleful. From then on, Reynard fell back until he was in rout. It took an abacus, borrowed from an adjacent laundry, to compute the grand total of the check. I handed over my wallet in a peach-colored haze underscored by the throb of distant tom-toms. Fortunately, I had had the presence of mind to tuck several bills into my shoe, for all I got back was a sweepstakes ticket and the celluloid calendar of a savings bank. Gastronomical wizard that he was, M. Reynard was a greater ironist.

*. . . she stared deep into my eyes and
told me I was cooking with gas.*

Speaking for myself, I would have preferred to cap our saturnalia
with a glass of ice-cold milk and a fervent assurance to my songbird
that I would call her up sometime, but Chloe was working on the
principle that if you stumble onto a mother lode, you stick until the
shovel is blunted. As she steered me up the carpeted stairs of the Club

Tornado, I wanly pleaded that my numerologist was expecting me at seven in the morning, that I was stricken with a return of blackwater fever contracted in the New Hebrides, that the Maffia had sworn to expunge me if I were seen in public.

"We'll just stay for the three-o'clock floor show," Chloe wheedled. "I've got to have a lemonade for this awful thirst." Room was cleared for us at ringside, a cigarette girl specially detailed to badger us with trayfuls of stale chocolates and gardenias, and a bonus promised the musicians if they whitened my hair by midnight. Notwithstanding these *douceurs,* Chloe was inclined to be sulky. "The joint is dead tonight," she said, pouting. "I don't see a soul I know."

My situation was more fortunate. Looking cursorily around, I managed to discover a good many familiar faces, all of them regarding me with strained attention. Some devilish magnetism had drawn together in our gallery three-quarters of my college class, most of the credit managers I had known in the past decade, a representative sprinkling of the arts and sciences, and the largest collection of copper's narks and tipsters ever assembled under one roof. They were particularly enthralled when my companion, her blood heated by four lemonades, twined her arms around my neck and posed for a candid-camera photographer. She subsequently became outraged at my refusal to buy the snapshots, but, as I pointed out very reasonably, I was bound to see them in the tabloids anyway.

I imagine the three-o'clock floor show was well under way by the time I got home, and if the professional hockey players I abandoned Chloe to continued their gallantries, she must have had a barrel of laughs. Only a rotter would be sufficiently base to sneak off as I did, and I confess I afterward ate the bitter bread of repentance. My regimen, in fact, was fairly unusual from the second my wife returned from Atlantic City. I began by eating crow and have since subsisted almost entirely on humble pie. It's filling, but nowhere as tasty as pressed duck with oranges.

Many a Slip

PIERRE BALMAIN's POLKADOT PETTICOAT PARISIENNES. We're as excited as a Broadway producer on opening night! For curtain's going up on our latest translation from the French — our play of petticoats with soft-gleaming rayon tissue faille! Advance notices are *rave* — we even have sell-out booking for our first order! It looks as if we've a hit on our hands with Balmain's leading lady of the fan-pleat ruffle and double-bowing — his ingénue of the cummerbund cinch and snow-dot showing! . . . [*Und so weiter.*]—*Russeks advertisement.*

> *SCENE: A hotel room in Wilmington, Delaware. It is in a state of some disorder as the curtain rises — newspapers strewn about, service trays cluttered with coffee cups and half-eaten chicken sandwiches, several partially empty Scotch bottles and glasses, ashtrays heaped with cigarette butts. On the davenport at left, hands interlaced behind his head and his eyes fixed unwinkingly on the ceiling, lies Costain, senior partner of Costain & Nudelman, lingerie manufacturers and sponsors of Cost-Nudel Creations. A day-old beard darkens his dyspeptic cheeks, and his nose is pinched with fatigue. Nudelman, his bald, hard-bitten associate, teeth clamped on a cigar, stands moodily staring out the window at a neon sign blinking on and off — an effect achieved by a stagehand with an electric torch concealed in the wings. Over the room hangs the unmistakable air of apprehensiveness typical of an out-of-town tryout. (Note: This last effect may be a trifle more difficult to achieve, but a good stage manager can do anything.)*

NUDELMAN (*whirling around*): Holy cats, quit pacing up and down, can't you?

COSTAIN: Who's pacing? I've been lying on this sofa the last ten minutes!

As the curtain rises . . .

NUDELMAN: Well, get off it. Pace up and down — do something, only stop looking like Svengali or Trilby or whoever it was. It's enough to turn a man's hair gray.

COSTAIN: You should worry, with that billiard ball *you've* got.

NUDELMAN (*darkly*): Now, look here, Costain, one more insinuendo about my scalp —

COSTAIN: All right, all right, skip it. We're both a little high-strung, I guess.

NUDELMAN: These tryouts are nothing but aggravation. The next underskirt I produce, we open cold in New York.

COSTAIN: Ah, that's what you always say. How can you find out what's wrong if you don't see it before an audience?

NUDELMAN: You call this bunch of rhubarb down here an audience?

COSTAIN: Well, they wear underwear, too. We're bound to get reactions.

NUDELMAN: Yeah, and strictly corny. They don't know from sophistication — the flounces, the eyelet embroidery, all the clever touches we beat our brains out to get into the script.

COSTAIN: Listen, that Noel Coward stuff never yet made a petticoat a smash. It's O.K. for the first-nighters in New York, but if you ask me, it's the meat-and-potatoes appeal — the old pull at the heartstrings — that'll put us over at the box office.

NUDELMAN (*gloomily*): Well, I wouldn't make book on these farmers. When our model gives with the prattfall on the dance floor and flashes her petticoat, they might figure it's an accident and yell.

COSTAIN: Just what we want — soften 'em up with some good rowdy slapstick. I remember I once broke in a pair of rompers in Cleveland —

NUDELMAN: Infants' wear is different. Young people go for low comedy.

COSTAIN: You can't be too broad. Look at Milady Underthins. They previewed three rayon slips in a row here in the Caprice Room and every one wowed the critics.

NUDELMAN: Theirs were all native-American folk slips — earthy, if you know what I mean. With an adaptation from the Hungarian, like ours, we should have opened in a more metropolitan pitch — Philly or New Haven.

COSTAIN (*hooting*): And have the whole wise mob from the needle trades there with their knives out? Those buzzards'd run right back to the Garment Center and spread the word we had a flop.

NUDELMAN (*consulting his watch*): I wish young Nirdlinger would get back here. I sent him downstairs to kind of mingle with the press and smell out how things are going.

COSTAIN: Say, I meant to speak to you about that boy. What makes him a press agent except the fact he's your nephew?

NUDELMAN: Just because the kid is only fifteen and wears knee pants —

COSTAIN: Oh, I know he's big for his age and all that —

NUDELMAN: You're damn right he is. He's been shaving for over two years.

COSTAIN: Still, it's a hundred and fifty a week on the payroll, and some of the backers are beginning to talk.

NUDELMAN: Let me ask you a question. Have you ever done the night spots with Teddy — the Stork, the Copa, the El Morocco?

COSTAIN: No, I can't say I have.

NUDELMAN: Well, if you want to see men fall all over theirselves, you just watch Lyons and Earl Wilson around Teddy. They're tongue-tied when he breezes in. He's like a god to them.

COSTAIN: Why?

NUDELMAN: Search me. Sheer personality, I suppose. All I know is, you never see little digs at Costain & Nudelman in their column, and to me that's worth the peanuts we pay him. Besides, show me another press agent who'll push a delivery truck in his spare time. I tell you, he's one in a million.

COSTAIN (*ungraciously*): Well, I wish somebody would tip him off that Edward Bernays don't wipe his nose on his sleeve. After all, how does it look for Cost-Nudel Creations —

NUDELMAN: That reminds me — I've been meaning to speak to you about something. Now, answer me honestly, Chick. Have I ever been unreasonable in my demands?

COSTAIN: I know that expression on your face. What are you driving at?

NUDELMAN: Time and again, I've given in to you, on the director, on casting —

COSTAIN: Come on, never mind the schmalz. Spit it out.

NUDELMAN: It's the producing credit. I've had my ear to the ground lately and there's a definite resistance on the public's part to the name of the firm.

COSTAIN (*dangerously*): So you were wondering if it wouldn't have more bite, maybe, if we switched it to Nudel-Cost Creations — is that it?

NUDELMAN (*taken aback*): How did you know?

COSTAIN: I've been making a study of weasels ever since our first bankruptcy.

NUDELMAN: I don't get you. We're not in the fur business.

COSTAIN: O.K., I'll blueprint it for you. Someone was writing "Nudel-Cost," "Nost-Cudel," "Nude-Costel," and a lot of other variations on that blotter over there.

NUDELMAN (*quickly*): It wasn't me.

COSTAIN: No, probably the woman who cleans up. (*The telephone rings. Nudelman springs to it. The eager expectancy on his face turns sour as he listens.*)

NUDELMAN (*banging down the receiver*): The desk. The designer's on his way up.

COSTAIN: After the way he carried on at rehearsal about changing the buttons to a zipper, you'd think he'd be ashamed to show himself.

NUDELMAN: Chick, we might as well face it. Anspacher can handle a camisole or a frilly nightgown, but a petticoat's over his head.

COSTAIN: What we need is a fresh slant. He's too close to it.

NUDELMAN: Mind you, I'm no writer, but I see a hundred places where it could stand brightening up — over the yoke, around the waistband, in the seams . . .

COSTAIN: I hate to call in somebody to doctor it, though. Once the news gets around Sardi's you're in trouble, you're practically in the hands of the jobbers.

NUDELMAN: I don't mean anyone with a big rep — I'd like to give some unknown with promise a chance. (*Casually.*) For instance, I heard of a brilliant kid up on the West Side. So far, he's only fooled around with panties, and I bet we could get him for tinfoil.

COSTAIN (*suspiciously*): What's his name?

NUDELMAN: What difference does that make? Rukeyser, I think — I don't recall exactly . . .

COSTAIN: Seems to me your wife has a nephew by that name.

NUDELMAN: Why — er — I believe there *is* a Rukeyser who's a distant relative. Just a coincidence.

COSTAIN: Have you ever thought of adopting me as your nephew? Then it would all be in the family. (*A knock at the door. Anspacher, the designer, enters excitedly. A slight unsteadiness hints that he has taken a dram or two.*)

NUDELMAN (*anxiously*): What's happened? Any news?

ANSPACHER: But colossal! It's the biggest thing that ever hit Wilmington!

COSTAIN: You're kidding!

ANSPACHER: You never saw such an uproar. The scouts from Rochester are using words like "Kuppenheimer." The hotel even had to call the police!

NUDELMAN (*paling*): The police? What for?

ANSPACHER: Why, to take our leading lady to the cooler; they're booking her now. Oh, that girl's a sweetheart! She played it to the hilt — she got values I never dreamt existed!

COSTAIN: For God's sake, stop brumbling! We didn't figure on the cops!

ANSPACHER: Darn right you didn't. (*Preening himself.*) That took imagination. Once I stumbled on the gimmick, everything fell into place.

NUDELMAN (*outraged*): You deliberately stuck in a new piece of business without consulting us?

ANSPACHER: Yes, sirree, and a dilly! I was knocking myself out for a twisteroo and it came to me in a flash before the performance — send her out in just the petticoat, with no dress at all!

NUDELMAN: It's madness! It violates every law of dramatic unity!

COSTAIN: And Delaware, too!

ANSPACHER: Wipe your chin, both of you. You've made sartorial history tonight and you don't know it.

NUDELMAN (*wringing his hands*): But laying it right in their laps like that . . . Where are the halftones, the shading, the Continental *soupçons* we're famous for?

ANSPACHER: Who cares? This is red-blooded, boffo entertainment for both sexes. You should have seen the men climbing on chairs to get a better view.

COSTAIN (*uneasily*): You — you say it really caused a sensation?

ANSPACHER: Terrific. You'll be all over the front page tomorrow, I guarantee you.

COSTAIN (*extracting a hat from closet*): Well, if it's as big as you say, I better bail out — I mean, I better get back to New York right away.

ANSPACHER: What for?

COSTAIN: To — to arrange additional financing. You know, for exploitation.

NUDELMAN (*following him to door*): Me, too. We don't want to get caught flat-footed with no exploitation.

ANSPACHER: But what am I supposed to do here?

NUDELMAN: You keep your eye on the creative angles. We'll tend to the business end.

ANSPACHER: Aren't you even going to wait for the reviews?

COSTAIN: No, no, you can phone 'em to us. Abba-dabba! (*They scurry out. Anspacher stares after them, then runs to door.*)

ANSPACHER: Hey! You forgot your suitcases! (*A pause. He turns back into room, pours himself a drink, and shrugs.*) Businessmen — huh!

CURTAIN

Cloudland Revisited

Into Your Tent I'll Creep

I FIRST read *The Sheik*, by E. M. Hull, during the winter of 1922-23, standing up behind the counter of a curious cigar store of which I was the night clerk, though I preferred the loftier designation of relief manager. I was, at the time, a sophomore at Brown University and had no real need of the job, as I was wealthy beyond the dreams of avarice. I had taken it solely because my rooms were a rallying point for the *jeunesse dorée* and were so full of turmoil and inconsequential babble that I was driven to distraction. Like Stevenson's Prince Florizel of Bohemia, who retired into Soho to conduct his cigar divan under the pseudonym of Theophilus Godall, I wanted anonymity and a quiet nook for study and speculation. I got enough of all these to last a lifetime, and, by discreet pilfering, sufficient cigarettes to impair the wind of the entire student body. Five months after I joined the enterprise, it was stricken with bankruptcy, the medical name for mercantile atrophy. To claim that I was wholly responsible would be immodest. I did what I could, but the lion's share of the credit belonged to Mr. Saidy, who owned the store.

Mr. Saidy was a hyperthyroid Syrian leprechaun, and a man of extraordinarily diversified talents. He was an accomplished portrait painter in the academic tradition, and his bold, flashy canvases, some of which were stored in our stockroom, impressed me as being masterly. John Singer Sargent and Zuloaga, whom he plagiarized freely, might have felt otherwise, but since neither was in the habit of frequenting our stockroom, Mr. Saidy was pretty safe from recrimination. In addition to the painting, playing the zither, and carving peach pits into monkeys to grace his watch chain, he was an inventor. He had patented a pipe for feminine smokers that held cigarettes in a vertical position and a machine for extracting pebbles from gravel roofs. Saidy's entry into the tobacco business had been motivated by a romantic conviction that he could buck the United Cigar Store combine, using its own methods. We issued coupons with all purchases, redeemable, according to their guarantee, for hundreds of valuable premiums. I saw only four of them in my tenure — an electric iron, a catcher's mitt, a Scout knife, and one of those mechanical blackamoors of the period that operated on victrola turntables and danced a clog to "Bambalina" or "The Japanese Sandman." At first, I was uneasy lest some patron present a stack of coupons he had hoarded and demand one of the other premiums listed. There was no basis for my anxiety. Mr. Saidy's prices were higher than our competitors', so the customers stayed away by the thousands, and the infrequent few who blundered in spurned the certificates as if they were infected.

At any rate, it was in this pungent milieu that I made the acquaintance of the immortal Lady Diana Mayo and the Sheik Ahmed Ben Hassan, and when, after a lapse of twenty-five years, I sat down recently to renew it, I was heavy with nostalgia. A goodish amount of water had gone over the dam in the interim and I was not at all sure Miss Hull's febrile tale would pack its original wallop. I found that, contrariwise, the flavor had improved, like that of fine old port. There is nothing dated about the book; the bromides, in fact, have a creaminess, a velvet texture, I am certain they lacked a quarter of a century ago. Any connoisseur knows that a passage like "She hated him with all the strength of her proud, passionate nature" or "I didn't love you when I took you, I only wanted you to satisfy the beast in me" acquires a matchless bouquet from lying around the cellar of a second-

63

hand bookshop. No slapdash artificial aging process can quite duplicate the tang. It must steep.

The opening paragraph of *The Sheik* is, possibly, the most superb
example of direct plot exposition in the language. Instead of fussing
over the table decorations and place cards, like so many novelists,
the author whisks open the door of the range and serves the soufflé
piping hot. In the very first line of the book, a disembodied voice asks
someone named Lady Conway whether she is coming in to watch
the dancing, and gets a tart reply: "I most decidedly am not. I thoroughly disapprove of the expedition of which this dance is the in-
auguration. I consider that even by contemplating such a tour alone
into the desert with no chaperon or attendant of her own sex, with
only native camel drivers and servants, Diana Mayo is behaving
with a recklessness and impropriety that is calculated to cast a slur
not only on her own reputation, but also on the prestige of her country. . . . It is the maddest piece of unprincipled folly I have ever
heard of."

That, I submit, is literary honesty of a high order, to say nothing
of a forensic style Cicero would have envied. It does not abuse the
reader's patience with a complex psychological probe of Diana's
youth, her awakening womanhood, her revolt against narrow social
conventions. It tells him with a minimum of flubdub that a madcap
miss is going to be loused up by Arabs and that there will be no ex-
changes or refunds. After making this speech, Lady Conway storms
off. It transpires that she has been addressing two gentlemen on the
veranda of the Biskra Hotel, an Englishman named Arbuthnot and
an unnamed American, who take an equally dim view of Diana's
temerity. Though both adore her, they are dismayed by her impru-
dence and heartlessness. "The coldest little fish in the world, without
an idea in her head beyond sport and travel," as Arbuthnot subsequently describes her, has been reared by her brother, Sir Aubrey,
a typical Du Maurier baronet, and obeys no bidding but her own
whim. When Arbuthnot leaves to beg a dance of the minx, his rival

The Sheik *by E. M. Hull*

speeds him with characteristic Yankee jocosity: "Run along, foolish moth, and get your poor little wings singed. When the cruel fair has done trampling on you I'll come right along and mop up the remains." I presume he punctuated this metaphoric nosegay with a jet of tobacco juice, slapped his thigh, and blew his nose into a capacious bandanna, but the text delicately makes no mention of it.

The singe, more of a second-degree burn, is administered in the garden, where Arbuthnot offers his hand to Diana, along with two memorable chestnuts to the effect that beauty like hers drives a man mad and that he won't always be a penniless subaltern. His avowals, however, go for nought, as does his plea that she abandon her foolhardy undertaking. She exhibits the same intransigence toward her brother the next evening, at the oasis to which he has escorted her. "I will do what I choose when and how I choose," she declares, turning up an already snub nose at his dark predictions, and, blithely promising to join him in New York, plunges into the trackless Sahara, accompanied only by a guide and several bodyguards. Had you or I written the story, our heroine would have cantered into Oran in due course with her nose peeling and a slight case of saddle gall. But sunburn alone does not create best-sellers, as Miss Hull well knew, and she has a bhoyo concealed in the dunes who is destined to put a crimp in Diana's plans, to phrase it very tactfully indeed.

For brevity's sake, we need not linger over the actual abduction of Diana by the Sheik; how her party is waylaid, how she is tempestuously swept onto his steed and spirited to his lair, must be tolerably familiar even to those too youthful to have seen it enacted on the screen by Agnes Ayres and Rudolph Valentino. The description of the desert corsair, though, as he takes inventory of his booty, attains a lyrical pitch current fiction has not surpassed: "It was the handsomest and cruelest face that she had ever seen. Her gaze was drawn instinctively to his. He was looking at her with fierce, burning eyes that swept her until she felt that the boyish clothes that covered her slender limbs were stripped from her, leaving the beautiful white body bare under his passionate stare." Under the circumstances, one cannot help feeling that her question, "Why have you brought me here?," betrays a hint of naïveté. The average man, faced with such a query, might have been taken unawares and replied weakly, "I forget," or "I guess I was overwhelmed by the sight of a pretty foot," but Ahmed's is no milksop answer: *"Bon Dieu! Are you not woman enough to know?"* This riposte so affected one spark I knew back in the early twenties that he used it exclusively thereafter in couch hammocks and canoes, but with what success is immaterial here. In the novel, at all events, the Arab chief, without further ado, works his sweet will of Diana, which explains in some measure why the book went into thirteen printings in eight months. I could be mistaken, of course; maybe it was only the sensuous lilt of the prose.

It may be asked, and reasonably, what the rest of the book deals with if such a ringing climax is reached on page 59. The story, simply, is one of adjustment; Ahmed Ben Hassan goes on working his sweet will of Diana with monotonous regularity, and she, in time, becomes reconciled to the idea. To be sure, she does not accept her martyrdom slavishly. She rages, threatens, implores, all to no purpose. Anguished, she demands why the Sheik has done this to her. "Because I wanted you," he returns coolly. "Because, one day in Biskra, four weeks ago, I saw you for a few moments, long enough to know that I wanted you. And what I want I take." All the scene needs to achieve perfection is a sardonic smile and a thin thread of smoke curling away from a monogrammed Turkish cigarette. These make their appearance in short order. Diana quaveringly asks when he will let her go. When he is tired of her, returns Ahmed with a sardonic smile, watching a thin thread of smoke curl away from a monogrammed Turkish cigarette. Small wonder every fiber of Diana's being cries out in protest.

"He is like a tiger," she murmurs deep into the cushions, with a shiver, "a graceful, cruel, merciless beast." She, in turn, reminds the Sheik of still another quadruped: "The easy swing of her boyish figure and the defiant carriage of her head reminded him of one of his own thoroughbred horses. . . . And as he broke them so would he

67

break her." The connubial relationship between horse and tiger, while a trifle perplexing from the biological point of view, settles into a surprisingly domestic pattern. Yet instead of rolling with the punches, so to speak, Diana willfully upsets the applecart by running away. Ahmed overtakes her, and it is when she is being toted home, slung across his pommel like a sack of oats, that she experiences the great awakening: "Why did she not shrink from the pressure of his arm and the contact of his warm, strong body? . . . Quite suddenly she knew — knew that she loved him, that she had loved him for a long time, even when she thought she hated him and when she had fled from him. . . . He was a brute, but she loved him, loved him for his very brutality and superb animal strength."

Naturally, it would be infra dig for any woman, especially a member of the British peerage, to bluntly confess a *béguin* for an obscure tribesman. Hence, there ensues an interval in which Diana plays cat-and-mouse with the chieftain, instead of horse-and-tiger, and arouses his wrath by her ladylike reserve. "*Bon Dieu!* . . . Has the vile climate of your detestable country frozen you so thoroughly that nothing can melt you?" he mutters thickly, contemning even the weather in his scorn. "I am tired of holding an icicle in my arms." Eventually, though, his dear nearness, scorching kisses, and equally fiery rhetoric produce a thaw, and Diana favors him with a few caresses of signal puissance. Strange to say, their effect is not precisely what one would imagine: " 'You go to my head, Diane,' he said with a laugh that was half anger, and shrugging his shoulders moved across the tent to the chest where the spare arms were kept, and unlocking it took out a revolver and began to clean it." Perhaps I was unduly stimulated, but after that torrid buildup, dilettantism with a pistol seemed no substitute for a volcano.

For all practical purposes, nevertheless, and halfway through her narrative, the author has proved to everyone's ennui that pride crumbles before primitive passion. Given another setting, the boy and girl could now trot around to the license bureau and legalize their union, but here, in addition to the lack of such facilities, there is still the embarrassing racial barrier confronting Diana. Bewitched as she is by her swain, she cannot quite blink at the fact that he is an Arab, a grubby little native by her social standards. To nullify this obstacle, the author puts some fairly ponderous machinery in motion. She introduces a lifelong chum of the Sheik, a novelist named the Vicomte Raoul de Saint Hubert, who also happens to be a crackajack surgeon. Then she causes Diana to be kidnaped by a rival sachem, from whom Ahmed rescues her, sustaining a grievous wound. As he hovers between life and death, watched over by the Vicomte and Diana, the gimmick is unveiled:

" 'His hand is so big for an Arab's,' she said softly, like a thought spoken aloud unconsciously.

" 'He is not an Arab,' replied Saint Hubert with sudden impatient vehemence, 'He is English.' " Yes, he continues, stunning Diana, if not the reader, his father is the Earl of Glencaryll. This news provokes a truly classic reaction from Diana: "Oh, now I know why that awful frown of Ahmed's has always seemed so familiar. Lord Glencaryll always frowns like that. It is the famous Caryll scowl." To soothe the literal-minded, there is a thirteen-page exegesis of the hero's background, complete with such reassuring details as a formal European education and a mother of noble Spanish birth. Diana doesn't really care, for she realizes that her woman's intuition, assisted by a bit of roughhouse from the Sheik, has guided her aright. When, on his recovery, he undergoes the mandatory change of heart and offers her freedom, the horse turns into a phoenix and rises reborn from the ashes: "She slid her arm up and around his neck, drawing his head down. 'I am not afraid,' she murmured slowly. 'I am not afraid of anything with your arms round me, my desert lover. Ahmed! Monseigneur!' "

If my examination of *The Sheik* did nothing else, it confirmed a suspicion I have been harboring for over two decades; namely, that the relief manager of a small cigar store in Providence about 1922 showed the most dubious literary taste of anyone I ever knew. To

69

add to his other defects — he was shiftless, scheming, and transparently dishonest — he was an incorrigible romantic, the type of addlepate that, in later life, is addicted to rereading the books of his youth and whining over their shortcomings. Altogether, an unattractive figure and, I fear, a hopelessly bad lot. But then I suppose there's no point in being too tough on the boy. You can't judge people like him and Diana Mayo by ordinary standards. They're another breed of cat.

Tuberoses and Tigers

BACK IN THE SUMMER of 1919, a fifteen-year-old youth at Riverside, Rhode Island, a watering place on the shores of upper Narragansett Bay, was a victim of a temporary but none the less powerful hallucination still referred to in southern New England as the "Riverside hallucination." For a space of three or four days, or until the effects of a novel called *Three Weeks*, by Elinor Glyn, had worn off, the boy believed himself to be a wealthy young Englishman named Paul Verdayne, who had been blasted by a searing love affair with a mysterious Russian noblewoman. His behavior during that period, while courteous and irreproachable to family and friends alike, was marked by fits of abstraction and a tendency to emit tragic, heartbroken sighs. When asked to sweep up the piazza, for instance, or bike over to the hardware store for a sheet of Tanglefoot, a shadow of pain would flit across his sensitive features and he would assent with a weary shrug. "Why not?" he would murmur, his lips curling in a bitter, mocking smile. "What else can life hold for me now?" Fortunately, his parents, who had seen him through a previous seizure in which he had identified himself with William S. Hart, were equipped to deal with his vagaries. They toned up his system with syrup of figs, burned his library card, and bought a second-hand accordion to distract him. Within a week, his distraction and that of the neighbors were so complete that the library card was hastily restored and the instrument disposed of — the latter no minor feat, as anyone knows who has ever tried to burn an accordion.

Not long ago, in a moment of nostalgia laced with masochism, it occurred to me to expose myself again to Miss Glyn's classic and see whether the years had diluted its potency. The only vivid recollection I preserved of the story was one of a sultry enchantress lolling on a tiger skin. I realized why the image had persisted when I ultimately tracked down a copy of the book. It was illustrated with scenes from the photoplay production Samuel Goldwyn gave it in 1924, and on the dust jacket, peering seductively at me across a snarling Indian man-eater, lay Aileen Pringle, mascaraed, braided, and palpitant with sex appeal. The very first page I sampled, before settling down to a leisurely feast, yielded a sweetmeat that corroborated my boyhood memory:

"A bright fire burnt in the grate, and some palest orchid-mauve silk curtains were drawn in the lady's room when Paul entered from the terrace. And loveliest sight of all, in front of the fire, stretched at full length was his tiger — and on him — also at full length — reclined the lady, garbed in some strange clinging garment of heavy purple *crêpe*, its hem embroidered with gold, one white arm resting on the beast's head, her back supported by a pile of the velvet cushions, and a heap of rarely bound books at her side, while between her lips was a rose not redder than they — an almost scarlet rose." It was very small wonder that when I originally read this passage, my breathing became shallow and I felt as if the Berea College choir were grouped in the base of my skull singing gems from Amy Woodford-Finden. Even the author seems to have had some fleeting compunction after writing it, for she went on hastily, "It was not what one would expect to find in a sedate Swiss hotel." If it thus affected Paul, you can guess what the impact was on Riverside, where our notion of barbaric splendor was a dish of fried eels.

Three Weeks touched off such a hullabaloo in England that, on its publication here, Miss Glyn wrote an exasperated preface for American readers, enjoining them to consider the spiritual rather that the fleshly aspects of her romance. "The minds of some human beings," she declared scornfully, "are as moles, grubbing in the earth for worms. . . . To such *Three Weeks* will be but a sensual record of passion." The real story, however, she explained, was the purifying effect upon a callow young Englishman of his gambol with a heroine whom Miss Glyn likened to a tiger (a simile she milked pretty exhaustively before the whistle blew) and described as "a great splendid nature, full of the passionate realization of primitive instincts, immensely cultivated, polished, blasé." She concluded her message with a request I am sure every novelist has longed to make at one time or another, and would if he had the courage: "And to all who read, I say — at least be just! and do not skip. No line is written without its having a bearing on the next, and in its small scope helping to make the presentment of these two human beings vivid and clear." I took the entreaty so much to heart that every last asterisk of *Three Weeks* was literally engraved on my brain, which, after two hundred and ninety pulsating pages, must have borne a striking resemblance to an old bath sponge peppered with buckshot.

The situation that obtains at the opening of Miss Glyn's fable, in all honesty, does not rank among the dizzier flights of the human imagination, but, in the vulgate of Vine Street, it's a springboard, and what the hell. Paul Verdayne, twenty-two years old, devastatingly handsome, and filthy with the stuff, has been dispatched by his elders on a tour of the Continent to cure his infatuation for a vicar's daughter. Nature, it appears, has been rather more bountiful.to Paul's body and purse than to his intellect; above the ears, speaking bluntly, the boy is strictly tapioca. As the curtain rises on what is to be the most electrifying episode of his life, he is discovered moodily dining at a hotel in Lucerne and cursing his destiny. Suddenly, there comes to his nostrils the scent of tuberoses, and a lady materializes at the next

table. At first, her exquisite beauty and sensuous elegance are lost

Three Weeks *by Elinor Glyn*

on him; then, as she proceeds to sup on caviar, a blue trout, *selle d'agneau au lait*, a nectarine, and Imperial Tokay, he perceives he is face to face with a thoroughbred, and the old familiar mixture of fire and ice begins stirring in his veins. Without any sign that she has noticed his presence, she glides out, overwhelming the young man with her figure: " 'She must have the smallest possible bones,' Paul said to himself, 'because it looks all curvy and soft, and yet she is as slender

73

as a gazelle.' " On a diet like the foregoing, I wouldn't give odds the lady would stay gazelle-slender perpetually, but perhaps her metabolism was as unusual as her charm. In any case, there is, as everyone is aware, a standard procedure for those smitten by mysterious sirens smelling of tuberoses; namely, to smoke a cigar pensively on the terrace, soothe one's fevered senses, and await developments. Paul faithfully adheres to the convention, and at length the lady, presumably having nullified gastritis with a fast Pepto-Bismol, slithers out onto her balcony and casts him a languishing glance. From that point on, it is *sauve-qui-peut* and prudent readers will do well to hold *Three Weeks* at arm's length, unless they want to be cut by flying adjectives.

In the ensuing forty-eight hours, Mme. Zalenska, as Paul ascertains her name to be from the register, plays a hole-and-corner game with her caballero, ogling him from behind beech trees, undulating past him in hotel corridors, and generally raising the deuce with his aplomb. Finally, when she has reduced him to the consistency of jellied consommé, she summons him to her suite for a short midnight powwow. The décor is properly titillating and, inevitably, includes Miss Glyn's favorite carnivore: "The lights were low and shaded, and a great couch filled one side of the room beyond the fireplace. Such a couch! covered with a tiger skin and piled with pillows, all shades of rich purple velvet and silk, embroidered with silver and gold — unlike any pillows he had ever seen before, even to their shapes." Paul, in his pitiable innocence, assumes he has been called to render some neighborly service, like installing a new Welsbach mantle or cobbling Zalenska's shoes. Actually, she wishes to warn him how lethal she is:

" 'Look at me,' she said, and she bent forward over him — a gliding feline movement infinitely sinuous and attractive. . . . Her eyes in their narrowed lids gleamed at him, seeming to penetrate into his very soul. . . . Suddenly she sprang up, one of those fine movements of hers, full of cat-like grace. 'Paul,' she said . . . and she spoke rather fast. 'You are so young, so young — and I shall hurt you — probably. Won't you go now — while there is yet time? Away from Lucerne,

back to Paris — even back to England. Anywhere away from me.' "
Had Paul, at this juncture, slipped into his reefer and whistled for
a fiacre, it might have saved both him and me considerable anguish,
but Miss Glyn's royalties certainly would have been stricken with
anemia. He therefore gallantly confides his heart into the lady's cus-
tody, snatches up an armful of tuberoses, and retires to the terrace
to stride up and down until dawn, soothing his fevered senses. This
is technically known in Publishers' Row as a tease play or the punch
retarded, a stratagem designed to keep the savages guessing.

In a brief pastoral interlude next day, idling about the lake in a
luxurious motor launch heaped with even stranger pillows and dialogue, Mme. Zalenska's mood is alternately maternal and bombas-
tic. "I wish to be foolish today, Paul," she says (a program she achieves
with notable success), "and see your eyes dance, and watch the light
on your curls." His ardor becomes well-nigh unendurable when, before teatime, she bends over him with the tantalizing comment "Great
blue eyes! So pretty, so pretty!," and he hoarsely begs her for instruc-
tion in the art of love. Her orotund answer sets the placid bosom of the
lake rippling: "Yes, I will teach you! Teach you a number of things.
Together we will put on the hat of darkness and go down into Hades.
We shall taste the apples of the Hesperides — we will rob Mercure
of his sandals — and Gyges of his ring." Just as the steam is bubbling
in Paul's gauges, however, Mme. Zalenska laughingly twists out of
his grasp, and another sequence ends with the poor *schlemiel* patrol-
ling his beat on the terrace. Whatever deficiencies of logic the author
may display on occasion, she surely cannot be accused of hurrying
her climax.

The spark that ignites the tinder, oddly enough, is a gift Paul purchases for his affinity — one of those characteristic souvenirs that
litter sedate Swiss hotels, a tiger skin. "It was not even dear as tigers
go, and his parents had given him ample money for any follies."
Sprawled out on it, strange greenish flames radiating from her pupils,
Mme. Zalenska goads the boy to the brink of neurasthenia by withholding the tuition she promised and proposing in its stead a literary

75

debauch. " 'Paul,' she cooed plaintively, 'tomorrow I shall be reason-able again, perhaps, and human, but today I am capricious and way-ward, and mustn't be teased. I want to read about Cupid and Psyche from this wonderful *Golden Ass* of Apuleius — just a simple tale for a wet day — and you and — me!' " By then, though, the lad in his own stumble-foot fashion has evolved a more piquant formula for passing a rainy day, and, with a prodigious amount of whinnying, purring, gurgling, and squealing, the education of Paul Verdayne swings into its initial phase.

How high a voltage the protagonists generate in the two remaining weeks of their affair, I cannot state with precision; the dial on my galvanometer burst shortly afterward, during a scene where they are shown cradled in a hotel on the Bürgenstock, exchanging baby talk and feeding each other great, luscious red strawberries. At Venice, to which they migrate for no stringent reason except that the author wanted to ring in a vignette of Mme. Zalenska biting Paul's ear lobes in a gondola, there is an account of their pleasure dome that deserves attention:

"The whole place had been converted into a bower of roses. The walls were entirely covered with them. A great couch of deepest red ones was at one side, fixed in such masses as to be quite resisting and firm. From the roof chains of roses hung, concealing small lights — while from above the screen of lilac-bushes in full bloom the moon in all her glory mingled with the rose-shaded lamps and cast a glam-our and unreality over the whole. . . . The dinner was laid on a table in the center, and the table was covered with tuberoses and stephan-otis, surrounding the cupid fountain of perfume."

And now the plot, hitherto snowed under by suchlike verdant *Katzenjammer,* refuses any longer to be denied. Awakening one noonday from his finals, which he has evidently passed *summa cum laude,* Paul finds a farewell note from his coach, setting forth that they must part forever, inasmuch as sinister forces in her background endanger both their lives. There have been sketchy intimations ear-lier that Mme. Zalenska is some sort of empress on a toot, or at least a margravine, and Paul has observed several dubious Muscovites tailing them around St. Mark's but, in his exaltation, has dismissed them as phantoms induced by overwork. The realization that he is henceforth cut off from postgraduate study exerts its traditional effect, and he goes down like a poled ox. By the time Sir Charles, his father, has arrived bearing cold compresses and beef tea, Paul lies between life and death, madly raving with brain fever. His convalescence, of course, follows the mandatory pattern — the Adriatic cruise aboard a convenient yacht, the Byronic soliloquies in the moonlight, and, back in England, the solitary rambles on the moors with the devoted rough-coated terrier. As time assuages his grief, a new Paul re-enters British society, older, fluent, worldly-wise. He prepares to stand for Parliament, scores a brilliant social success: "He began to be known as someone worth listening to by men, and women hung on his words. . . . And then his complete indifference to them piqued and allured them still more. Always polite and chivalrous, but as aloof as a mountain top." I don't want to sound vindictive, but can you imagine asking a man like that to scoot over to the hardware store for ten cents' worth of fly rolls? That's the kind of thing I was up against on Narragansett Bay thirty years ago.

The rest of *Three Weeks* is soon told, although not soon enough, frankly, by Miss Glyn, who consumes fifty marshmallow-filled pages to accomplish what she might have in two. After an endless amount of palaver, she discloses that Paul's and Zalenska's seminar has resulted in a bonny little cub and that, for all their pledges of devotion, the lovers are never reunited. The latter oversight is excused by as nimble a washup as you will find anywhere in the post-Victorian novel: "Everyone knows the story which at the time convulsed Europe. How a certain evil-living King, after a wild orgie of mad drunkenness, rode out with two boon companions to the villa of his Queen, and there, forcing an entrance, ran a dagger through her heart before her faithful servants could protect her. And most people were glad, too, that this brute paid the penalty of his crime by his own death — his worthless life choked out of him by the Queen's devoted

Kalmuck groom." This salubrious housecleaning elevates the tot to the throne, and as the book ends, Paul kneels in the royal chapel before the boy, quivering with paternal pride and chauvinism: "The tiny upright figure in its blue velvet suit, heavily trimmed with sable, standing there proudly. A fair, rosy-cheeked, golden-haired English child . . . And as he gazed at his little son, while the organ pealed out a Te Deum and the sweet choir sang, a great rush of tenderness filled Paul's heart, and melted forever the icebergs of grief and pain."

A few hours after finishing *Three Weeks*, there came to me out of the blue a superb concept for a romantic novel, upon which I have been laboring like a demon ever since. In essence, it is the story of an incredibly handsome and wealthy youth of forty-four whose wife and children, dismayed by his infatuation for servant-girl literature, pack him off to Switzerland. There he meets and falls in love with a ravishing twenty-three-year-old girl, half tigress and half publisher. The tigress in her fascinates him at the same time that the publisher revolts him, and out of this ambivalence, so to speak, grows the conflict. . . . But why am I telling you all this? I can see you're really not listening.

Sodom in the Suburbs

THE CLOSEST I ever came to an orgy, aside from the occasion in Montparnasse twenty years ago when I smoked a cigarette purported to contain hashish and fainted dead away after two puffs, was at a student dance at Brown around 1922. I did not suspect it was an orgy until three days later; in fact, at the time it seemed to me decorous to the point of torpor and fully consonant with the high principles of the Brown Christian Association, under whose auspices it was held. Attired in a greenish Norfolk jacket and scuffing the massive bluchers with perforated toe caps and brass eyelets considered *de rigueur* in that period, I spent the evening buffeting about in the stag line, prayerfully beseeching the underclassmen I knew for permission to cut in on their women and tread a few measures of the Camel Walk. At frequent intervals, noisily advertising an overpowering thirst, I retired to a cloakroom with several other blades and choked down a minute quantity of gin, warmed to body heat, from a pocket flask. Altogether, it was a strikingly commonplace experience, and I got to bed without contusions and stayed there peaceably riffling through *Jurgen* and humming snatches of "Avalon."

The following Sunday, I learned, to my astonishment, that I had been involved in a momentous debauch; the campus reeked of a scandal so sulphurous that it hung over our beanies like a nimbus for the rest of the academic year. In blazing scareheads, the Hearst Boston *American* tore the veil from the excesses tolerated at Brown University dances. At these hops, it thundered, were displayed a depravity and libertinism that would have sickened Petronius and made Messalina hang her head in shame. It portrayed girls educated at the best finishing schools, crazed with alcohol and inflamed by ragtime, oscillating cheek to cheek with young ne'er-do-wells in raccoon coats and derbies. Keyed up by savage jungle rhythms, the *abandonnés* would then reel out to roadsters parked on Waterman Street, where frat pins were traded for kisses under cover of darkness. Worst of all, and indicative of the depths to which the Jazz Age had reduced American womanhood, was the unwritten law that each girl must check her corset before the saturnalia. Painting a picture that combined the more succulent aspects of the Quatz' Arts Ball and a German officers' revel in occupied Belgium — two types of wassail long cherished by Hearst feature writers — the writer put all his metaphors in one basket and called upon outraged society to apply the brakes, hold its horses, and retrieve errant youth from under the wheels of the juggernaut. It was a daisy, and whoever did the pen drawings that enhanced it had given a lot of thought to the female bust.

I was poignantly reminded of that epoch and its turbulent escapades the other afternoon as I sat puffing a meerschaum and turning the leaves of a novel called *Flaming Youth,* which attained an immense vogue about that time not only with the general public but with the owner of the meerschaum. The book was hailed by press and pulpit as a blistering, veracious study of the moral chaos prevalent in the upper brackets, and it was popularly believed that its author, ostensibly a physician writing under the pseudonym of Warner Fabian, was, in reality, a top-drawer novelist. If he was, he successfully managed to conceal it; his style, at once flamboyant, euphuistic, and turgid, suggested nothing quite so much as melted marzipan. Fabian was plainly determined to leave no scintilla of doubt that he was a neophyte, for he wrote a windy foreword affirming it, the final segment of which seems to me to prove his claim incontestably: "To the woman of the period thus set forth, restless, seductive, greedy, discontented, craving sensation, unrestrained, a little morbid, uneducated, sybaritic, following blind instincts and perverse fancies, slack of mind as she is trim of body, neurotic and vigorous, a worshiper of tinseled gods at perfumed altars, fit mate for the hurried, reckless, and cynical man of the age, predestined mother of — what manner of being?: To Her I dedicate this study of herself." I don't know why, but I got the feeling from the foregoing that the doctor was a precise and bloodless little creep with a goatee I would dearly love to tweak. I could just see him whipping to his feet at a panel of nose specialists, removing his pince-nez with maddening deliberation, and beginning, "With the permission of the chair, I should like to amplify Dr. Westerphal's masterly orientation of the Eustachian tubes."

The fictional family chosen by the author to typify the decadence of the twenties is named Fentriss, resident in a well-to-do Westchester or Long Island suburb called Dorrisdale. Stripped of its gingerbread, the story concerns itself with the amours of the three Fentriss daughters, Constance, Dee, and Pat, whose adolescence has been colored by their mother's reckless hedonism. She, while delectable, sounds from Fabian's thumbnail description very much like an early Cubist portrait by Picasso: "She was a golden-brown, strong, delicately rounded woman, glowing with an effect of triumphant and imperishable youth. Not one of her features but was faulty by strict artistic tenets; even the lustrous eyes were set at slightly different levels." Mona Fentriss's life of self-indulgence has done more than throw her features out of whack; in the opening stanza, we see her being told by her physician and devoted admirer, Dr. Robert Osterhout, that there are fairies at the bottom of her aorta and that her days are numbered. Osterhout is a gruff, lovable character in the best medico-literary tradition: "Like a bear's, his exterior was rough, shaggy, and seemed not to fit him well. His face was irregularly square, homely, thoughtful, and humorous." Ever the heedless pagan, Mona turns a deaf ear to the voice of doom and, over the single shaker- ful of cocktails the doctor has restricted her to daily, confesses no remorse for her numerous extramarital affairs. Her husband, she con- fides, is equally unconcerned at her peccadilloes ("They say he's got a Floozie now, tucked away in a cozy corner somewhere"), and it is a lead-pipe cinch that, given this profligate environment and dubious heredity, the Fentriss girls are going to cut some pretty spectacular didos once the saxophones start sobbing.

We get our first peep at the dissipation extant in the household at a party thrown by Mona shortly afterward and characterized as fol- lows: "The party was a Bingo. . . . Lovely, flushed, youthful, regnant in her own special queendom, Mona Fentriss sat in the midst of a circle of the older men, bandying stories with them in voices which were discreetly lowered when any of the youngsters drew near. It was the top of the time." Pat, the youngest daughter, has been considered too young to attend, but she abstracts a dinner dress from one of her sisters and eavesdrops in the shrubbery. A furious crap game rages in the breakfast nook, furtive giggles emanate from parked cars, and, in the conservatory, Pat overhears her mother holding an equivocal duologue with Sidney Rathbone, an elderly but distinguished Bal- timorean of nearly forty. A moment later, a glass of home brew is rudely forced to Pat's lips; as she recoils from the searing liquid, she is kissed violently and an insinuating voice pleads in her ear,

"Come on, sweetie! We'll take a fifty-mile-an-hour dip into the landscape. The little boat [automobile, in the argot of '22] can go some." Much to Pat's discomfiture, however, her mother intercedes, routs the befuddled Princetonian besieging her daughter, and packs her off to bed. But the damage has been done, and, as Fabian darkly observes, tucking back his sleeves and preparing to fold a spoonful of cantharides into his already piquant meringue, that first smacker is the one a girl never forgets.

The narrative jogs along uneventfully for a spell, enlivened by a couple of minor scandals: Mrs. Fentriss shacks up briefly at a hotel called the Marcus Groot, in Trenton, with the aforesaid Sidney Rathbone, and Constance, the eldest daughter, underestimates her resistance to Bacardi, passes out in her cavalier's room, and is forced to still gossiping tongues by marrying him. A quick time lapse now enables the author to dispose of the exuberant Mrs. Fentriss and dress the stage for the entrance of the hero, Cary Scott, a former flame of hers encountered on a trip abroad. The description of Scott, clad in a sealskin coat and astrakhan cap, sufficiently explains why he sets the Fentriss girls by the ears: "No woman would have called him handsome. His features were too irregular, and the finely modeled forehead was scarred vertically with a savagely deep V which mercifully lost itself in the clustering hair, a testimony to active war service. There was confident distinction in his bearing, and an atmosphere of quiet and somewhat ironic worldliness in voice and manner. He looked to be a man who had experimented much with life in its larger meaning and found it amusing but perhaps not fulfilling." Nor does he become less glamorous when he admits, in the cultivated accents of one more at home in French than in his native tongue, that he has lived much out of the world: "The East; wild parts of Hindustan and northern China; and then the South Seas. I have a boy's passion for travel." This suave customer, understandably, makes the youths at the Dorrisdale country club seem pretty loutish to radiant, eighteen-year-old Pat, and she falls headlong. He reciprocates in flippant, half-serious fashion, regarding her as merely another spoiled flapper; be-

Flaming Youth *by Warner Fabian*

sides, like all distinguished men of the world with deep Vs, he is chained to an impossible wife in Europe, and even the most beef-witted reader must appreciate what plot convulsions are required to reconcile such opposites.

An episode of mixed nude bathing next ensues to blueprint the élan of the younger set, in the course of which the guests, emboldened by draughts of a potation called a "submarine cocktail," cavort about a pool in a thunderstorm pinching each other. In consequence, Dee, the second Fentriss girl, weds a rotter; Cary Scott goes back to Paris; and Pat is sent away to school. When Cary sees her on his return, she has burgeoned into what he terms a *"petite gamine,"* a phrase she does not understand; evidently she has been attending some technical school, like the Delehanty Institute. "You know what a gamin is?" he inquires. "*Gamine* is the feminine. But there's a suggestion in it of something more delicate and fetching; of verve, of − of *diablerie*." Leave it to those expatriates to explain one French word with another; he might at least have gone on to tell her that *diablerie* was derived from the game of diavolo, just making its appearance in the smarter salons of the Faubourg St. Honoré. Anyhow, he takes her to a concert, where Tchaikovsky's Fifth Symphony makes them kinspirits, and, swept away by the bassoons, kisses her. Almost instantly, though, he feels the lash of conscience and excoriates himself in a noteworthy soliloquy: "It was incredible; it was shameful; it was damnable; but this child, this *petite gamine*, this reckless, careless, ignorant, swift-witted, unprincipled, selfish, vain, lovable, impetuous, bewildering, seductive, half-formed girl had taken his heart in her two strong, shapely woman-hands, and claimed it away from him − for what? A toy? A keepsake? A treasure? What future was there for this abrupt and blind encounter of his manhood and her womanhood?" Follows a thirty-one-page renunciation jam-packed with rough tenderness, eyes shadowed with pain, and germane claptrap, and Cary vamooses to California. There was one thing you could be reasonably sure of in any novel published between 1915 and 1925: the minute the protagonists got within biting distance of each other, one of them was fated to board a boat or choo-choo within seventy-two hours.

As might be anticipated, Pat thereupon reacts in accordance with the protocol governing the broken-hearted and plunges into a mad round of pleasure, careering around the countryside at 40 m.p.h. in sleek Marmon runabouts, ingesting oceans of hooch, and inhaling straw-tipped Melachrinos. When Cary, despite himself, is drawn back to her, he finds her more provocative than ever, a disturbing amalgam of elf, kitten, and bacchante: "She shook the gleamy mist of her hair about her face, gave a gnomish twist to body and neck, and peered sidelong at him from out the tangle." His punctilio holds fast until someone next door idly starts plucking a fiddle, and then hell breaks loose again: "The long, thrilling, haunted wind-borne prayer of the violin penetrated the innermost fiber of her, mingling there with the passionate sense of his nearness, swaying her to un-defined and flashing languors, to unthinkable urgencies. . . . With a cry he leapt to her, clasped her, felt her young strength and lissome grace yield to his enfoldment. . . . Outside the great wind possessed the world, full of the turbulence, the fever, the unassuaged desire of Spring, the *allegro furioso* of the elements, and through it pierced the unbearable sweetness of the stringed melody."

Well, sir, that would seem to be it. By all the ordinary rules of physiology and pulp fiction, Pat and Cary should have been allowed at this juncture to retire tranquilly to the Fruit of the Loom without let or hindrance and frisk as they pleased. But Fabian, in inverse ratio to the reader, is just getting interested in his characters and figuring out new ways to frustrate them. They keep everlastingly melting into scorching embraces and springing apart the moment a rapproche-ment impends between them. She wants, he don't want; he wants, she don't want — your exasperation eventually reaches such a pitch that you would like to knock their heads together and lock them up in a motel with a copy of van der Velde's *Ideal Marriage*. The subplot bumbles in at intervals, adding to the general obfuscation a thwarted intrigue involving Dee Fentriss and a British electrician stylishly named Stanley Wollaston. At last, with the rueful conclusion: "We're terrible boobs, Cary. . . . Let's stop it" — a suggestion hardly calculated to provoke a quarrel with me — Pat sends her lover away to think things out and pins her affections on Leo Stenak, a brilliant violinist. This peters out when she discovers that he washes infrequently ("She forgot the genius, the inner fire; beheld only the outer shell, uncouth, pulpy, nauseous to her senses"), and she becomes affianced to Monty Standish, a Princeton football idol whose personal dainti-ness is beyond reproach. And then, in a smashing climax, so suspense-ful that the least snore is liable to disrupt the delicate balance of his

yarn, Fabian deftly turns the tables. Cary appears with the providential news that his wife has freed him, lips settle down to an unin-
terrupted feast, and, oblivious of the dead and dying syntax about
them, the lovers go forth in search of Ben Lindsey and a companion-
ate marriage.

It may be only a coincidence, but for a whole day after rereading
Flaming Youth, my pupils were so dilated that you would have sworn
I had been using belladonna. My complexion, though somewhat rud-
dier, recalled Bartholomew Sholto's in *The Sign of the Four* as he lay
transfixed by an aboriginal dart that fateful night at Pondicherry
Lodge. Luckily, I managed to work out a simple, effective treatment
I can pass on to anyone afflicted with star-dust poisoning. All you
need is an eyedropper, enough kerosene to saturate an average three-
hundred-and-thirty-six-page romance, and a match. A darkened room,
for lying down in afterward, is nice but not absolutely essential. Just
keep your eyes peeled, your nose clean, and avoid doctors and novels
written by doctors. When you're over forty, one extra bumper of
overripe beauty can do you in.

How Ruritanian Can You Get?

I TRUST I may be spared the accusation of being an old fogy, but prices
these days are really unconscionable. As recently as 1918, it was possible for a housewife in Providence, where I grew up, to march into
a store with a five-cent piece, purchase a firkin of cocoa butter, a
good second-hand copy of Bowditch, a hundredweight of quahogs,
a shagreen spectacle case, and sufficient nainsook for a corset cover,
and emerge with enough left over to buy a balcony admission to *The
Masquerader,* with Guy Bates Post, and a box of maxixe cherries.
What the foregoing would cost her today I shudder to think; one

fairly affluent Rhode Islander I met last summer confessed to me that he simply could not afford a pat of cocoa butter for his nose, and as for corset covers, his wife just threw up her hands. Along with the necessities of life, labor in the early twenties was unbelievably abundant and cheap. Imagine, for example, being able to hire the recording secretary of the Classical High School debating society — a man whose mordant irony reminded his auditors of Disraeli and Brann the Iconoclast, although he had scarcely turned sixteen — to sift your ashes and beat your carpets at thirty cents an hour. Even I find it almost too fantastic to credit, and, mind you, I *was* the recording secretary.

It was while sifting and beating about the home of a Providence chatelaine one spring afternoon that I came into possession of a book that was to exert a powerful influence on me for a long time to come. In a totally inexplicable burst of generosity, my employer, an odious Gorgon in brown bombazine, presented me with an armload of novels that had been moldering in her storeroom more than a decade. Among them, I recall, were such mellow favorites as *V.V.'s Eyes,* by Henry Sydnor Harrison; *Satan Sanderson* and *A Furnace of Earth,* by Hallie Erminie Rives; William J. Locke's *The Beloved Vagabond; The Goose Girl,* by Harold MacGrath; and *Graustark,* George Barr McCutcheon's best-seller published at the turn of the century. Curled up in my den on a mound of pillows covered with the flags of all nations, I consumed the lot in a single evening, buffeted by emotional typhoons so tempestuous that the family twice broke down the door to discover the cause of my spectacular groans and sighs. The one that gave me the most lasting belt was *Graustark.* Not since Janvier's masterly *In the Sargasso Sea,* a thrilling saga of the adventures of two boys mired in the North Atlantic kelp, had I read a story charged with such arresting characters and locales, such bravado and rollicking high humor. As I sped with Grenfall Lorry from our Western plains to the crags of Edelweiss in his mad pursuit of the beauteous Miss Guggenslocker, it seemed to me that for sheer plot invention and felicity of phrase McCutcheon must forever dwarf any other novelist in the language. For at least a fortnight afterward, I patterned myself on his

S.J. (circa 1918) reads Graustark
by George Barr McCutcheon

insouciant hero, spouting jaunty witticisms like "You tell 'em, goldfish, you've been around the globe" and behaving with a nervous hilarity that sent acquaintances scuttling around corners at my approach.

Several months back, I was sequestered over a rainy weekend in a cottage at Martha's Vineyard whose resources consisted of a crokinole board and half a dozen romances of the vintage of those mentioned above. By an electrifying coincidence, the first one I cracked turned out to be *Graustark*. Our reunion, like most, left something to be desired. I do not think I had changed particularly; perhaps my reflexes were a little less elastic, so I often had to backtrack forty or fifty pages to pick up the thread, and occasionally I fell into a light reverie between chapters, but in the main my mind had lost none of its vacuity and was still as supple as a moist gingersnap. *Graustark,* on the other hand, had altered almost beyond recognition. During the twenty-eight intervening years, it was apparent, some poltergeist had sneaked in and curdled the motivation, converted the hero into an insufferable jackanapes, drawn mustaches on the ladies of the piece, and generally sprinkled sneeze powder over the derring-do. Of course, mine was a purely personal reaction, and the average bobby-soxer reading it for the first time would doubtless disagree, but, as they say on the outer boulevards, *chacun à son* goo.

The principals of *Graustark* — a wealthy young American sportsman named Grenfall Lorry and a fair blue-blood traveling, under the laborious incognito of Sophia Guggenslocker, with her aunt and uncle — meet at the outset in this country aboard a transcontinental express, a setting subsequently much favored by the Messrs. Ambler, Greene, and Hitchcock in their entertainments. Apart from this footling resemblance, though, McCutcheon lacks any visible kinship with those masters of suspense; for instance, he jealously withholds the secret of his heroine's identity for a hundred and fifty-five glutinous pages, long past the point where you care whether she is the Princess Yetive of Graustark or Hop-o'-My-Thumb. Lorry is the type of popinjay who was ubiquitous in the novels of the nineteen-hundreds but has largely disappeared from current fiction. He has been everywhere, done everything; he has an income "that had withstood both the Maison Dorée and a dahabeah on the Nile," and, as the author explains in as natty a syllepsis as you will find in a month's hard search through Fowler, "he had fished through Norway and hunted in India, and shot everything from grouse on the Scottish moors to the rapids above Assouan." He is, in fine, a pretty speedy customer, and the photographs of him in the text, taken from the play version, confirm it. Even if his toupee is askew and his pepper-and-salt trousers are so baggy in the seat as to suggest that he is concealing a brace of grouse, Grenfall Lorry is a cove to be reckoned with.

In accordance with the usual ground rules, Miss Guggenslocker's dimples effectively snare Lorry as their train chuffs out of Denver, and he sets himself to further their acquaintance through a number of ruses too roguish to be exhumed. That she is not wholly oblivious is evidenced as he vaults aboard the carriage after a brief stop: "There was an expression of anxiety in her eyes as he looked up into them, followed instantly by one of relief. . . . She had seen him swing upon the moving steps and had feared for his safety — had shown in her glorious face that she was glad he did not fall beneath the wheels." This display of feeling, while not quite tantamount to an invitation to creep into her sleeping bag, nevertheless heartens Lorry and he perseveres. His opportunity comes when the two of them, through an elephantine convolution of the plot, are temporarily marooned in a mining town in the Alleghenies. Frenziedly careering through mountain passes in an ancient stage, Lorry assists the lady in rejoining the train, learns she is a Graustarkian, and, in the course of their intimacy, revs himself up to a rather alarming pitch of emotion: "Her sweet voice went tingling to his toes with every word she uttered. He was in a daze, out of which sung the mad wish that he might clasp her in his arms, kiss her, and then go tumbling down the mountain." Safe again on the flier, Miss Guggenslocker commends him to her party for his gallantry but in the next breath dashes his hopes; she is about to sail for home on the *Kaiser Wilhelm der Grosse*. They share an idyllic afternoon of sightseeing in Washington (during which they glimpse President Cleveland taking a constitutional, a sight that mysteriously evokes a ringing eulogy on our democratic process) and part with Lorry's fierce assurance that he will someday follow her to Graustark — possibly the most paltry bon-voyage gift ever tendered a girl in the history of the American novel.

For the sake of brevity, a virtue McCutcheon cannot be said to have held in idolatry, we may dust lightly over Lorry's *Sturm und Drang* in the months that follow, his departure for Graustark, and his arrival in Edelweiss, the capital of that country, in the company of Harry Anguish, an ex-Harvard classmate as painfully blithe as himself. The profundity and broad social tolerance of the latter can be gauged from his reactions as they near Edelweiss, the capital: "I'll be glad when we can step into a decent hotel, have a rub, and feel like white men once more. I am beginning to feel like those dirty Slavs and Huns we saw 'way back there." The search for Lorry's inamorata leads them to the chief of police, a Baron Dangloss, whose name appears to be a suspicious hybrid of Danglers, in *The Count of Monte Cristo*, and Pangloss, the philosopher of *Candide*, though he has none of the savor of either. Dangloss foxily pretends not to know who Miss Guggenslocker is, and Lorry is on the verge of defenestrating himself when he spies her in a royal carriage guarded by footmen and outriders. To his dismay, she drives on with only the most casual sign of recognition, but inside the hour a groom arrives with a note bidding him to call on her the next day. As Lorry, still without any suspicion of her actual identity, ponders these baffling developments, his colleague offers a deduction right out of 221B Baker Street. "I'll tell you what I've worked out during the past two minutes," he announces portentously. "Her name is no more Guggenslocker than mine is. She and the uncle used that name as a blind." It is plain as day that there are no flies on Harry Anguish. Those little black specks you see are merely vertigo.

Before the scheduled meeting can take place, the plot suddenly puts forth a series of tendrils and strangles the reader like a tropical liana. Strolling under the castle walls that evening, Lorry and Anguish overhear a design to abduct Princess Yetive. Conveniently for them, the conspirators couch it in a language they can grasp: "We must be careful to speak only in English. There are not twenty people in Edelweiss who understand it, but the night has ears." Ensues a sequence bristling with muffled oaths, judo, and chloroform, at the end of which Lorry bilks the kidnapers and discovers Miss Guggenslocker to be the Princess Yetive. What with the impact of this thunderbolt and a felonious blow on the sconce, he falls senseless, and spends the following chapter being nursed back to health by his royal sweetheart. Instead of their developing the rapport one would normally expect, though, it now transpires that Yetive's throne stands between the lovers; their dialogue resounds with echoing periods like "I find a princess and lose a woman!" and "The walls which surround the heart of a princess are black and grim, impenetrable when she defends it, my boasting American." There is, in addition, a whole labyrinthine complex of political reasons why Graustark girl and Melican boy may not fuse at the moment, and, reining his narrative back on its haunches, Mc-Cutcheon proceeds to catalogue them with all the exhaustive detail of a Gibbon or a Macaulay.

Boiled down to their marrow, it seems that Graustark, in consequence of a disastrous war with Axphain, a bordering state, owes its neighbors twenty-five million gavvos it cannot pay. Bankruptcy and dishonor face the nation, and Yetive, who is *de-facto* ruler, is nearly beside herself with anxiety. "Her Royal Highness," Lorry is told by Count Halfont, her uncle, "spent the evening with the ministers of finance and war, and her poor head, I doubt not, is racking from the effects of the consultation. These are weighty matters for a girl to have on her hands." Eventually, Yetive's head stops racking, and she agrees to marry Lorenz of Axphain to lift the mortgage, notwithstanding Lorry's reproaches and tantrums. The second the betrothal is announced, a chain of fictional firecrackers begins exploding. Lorenz of Axphain, a debauchee and wastrel, utters a coarse jape about Yetive in a saloon, sustains a haymaker from Lorry, and demands satisfaction under the code. Just before the duel, he is found murdered; Lorry is accused, on circumstantial evidence, and is flung into poky. His release is effected by a bosomy hussar with a piping voice and a strangely reminiscent perfume, who persists in shielding her face as they flee in a carriage. Lorry, hardly what might be called the intuitive sort, at last surrenders to curiosity and insists on seeing his benefactor's features: "Below the arm that hid the eyes and nose he saw parted lips and a beardless, dainty chin; above, long, dark tresses strayed in condemning confusion. The breast beneath the blue coat heaved convulsively." In the next moment, the soldier melts into the fugitive's arms and the prose into nougat: "The lithe form quivered and then became motionless in the fierce, straining embrace; the head dropped upon his shoulder, his hot lips caressing the burning face and pouring wild, incoherent words into the little ears. 'You! You!' he cried, mad with joy. 'Oh, this is Heaven itself! My brave darling! Mine forever — mine forever! You shall never leave me now! Drive on! Drive on!' he shouted to the men outside, drunk with happiness. 'We'll make this journey endless. I know you love me now — I know it! God, I shall die with joy!' " The degree of fever this passage induced in me at sixteen was so intense that steam issued from my ears and I repeatedly had to sluice myself down with ice water. At forty-four, while it is true my breathing grew increasingly stertorous, it was marked by a rhythmical whistling sound, and had a cigarette not fallen on my chest in the nick of time, I would still be hibernating on Martha's Vineyard, and nobody the wiser.

It would be permissible to suppose that Lorry and his sugarplum are now ready for the orange blossoms and flat silver, but anyone who did so would indulge in wishful thinking. Yetive, stashing her beau at a monastery until he cools off officially and personally, returns to confront problems of state. The enraged Axphainians insist on Harry Anguish's being held as a hostage, and finally propose to remit the national tribute if Lorry is captured and executed. Meanwhile, as if to further befog his lens, the author whips in yet another complication, a satanic toad of a monarch named Gabriel of Dawsbergen, likewise hungry for Yetive and prepared to square the debt in exchange for her hand. The whole fragrant chowder comes to a boil when Lorry steals back to visit the Princess, is surprised in her boudoir by the aforementioned Gabriel, and is blackmailed into giving himself up. Ultimately, in a climactic scene that travels with the speed of library paste, Gabriel is publicly unmasked by Anguish as both the assassin of Lorenz and the engineer of the scheme to snatch Yetive, and Axphain generously agrees to laugh off the horrid old indemnity that has been animating the plot. Amid popular rejoicing, Yetive persuades her ministers to accept Lorry as prince consort, Anguish and a countess he has been spoony on pair off, and as the book slips from one's nerveless fingers the foursome leaves in a shower of ennui for Washington, D.C.

I forget exactly what Eastern religion it is, whether Buddhism or Taoism, that holds that life is entirely a series of repetitions and that everything we experience has happened before. If I ever doubted it, it was proved overpoweringly that afternoon on the Vineyard. Within ten minutes after I finished rereading *Graustark*, a sensitive young kid on the order of Barbara LaMarr knocked timidly on the door and offered to sift my ashes or beat the carpets for a simply laughable fee. Inasmuch as I was only a house guest, I had no need of her services, but I presented her with a novel that had been moldering on my chest all day, and you've never seen anyone so bowled over. Poor thing broke down, and if I hadn't caught her in time, I believe she would have fainted; upon my soul I do. I was pretty moved myself — one of those cases where the gift enriches the giver as well, I guess. Oh, pshaw, you mustn't mind my running on. I act this way every time I get near one of those mythical kingdoms.

Lady, Play Your Endocrines

IN THE LATTER half of 1925, when the spirit of François Villon still hovered over the Jumble Shop and no poetry evening was complete without Eli Siegel declaiming "Hot Afternoons Have Been in Montana," I shared with another impecunious prospector and fellow-alumnus from Brown a cavernous, dingy room on West Eighth Street, in the Village. Four flights up and colder than the Kirghiz Steppe, it was nevertheless pervaded by a tropical effluvium from the dry cleaner's on the ground floor and commanded an unobstructed view of five restaurants neither of us could afford to patronize. We took our meals, to use a very loose designation, at a cruller shop down the block, and while we succeeded in sustaining life, I have ever since managed to view doughnuts with a measure of stoicism. Montague Adair, my roommate, was one of those unique personalities whose exteriors are as distinguished as their names. His classic features, seemingly chiseled of purest Parian marble, sable hair that put the raven's wing to shame, and an air of Beardsleyesque melancholy had already devastated innumerable coeds, and, to judge from the lipsticks and bobby pins strewn about when one returned from an enforced evening's stroll, he was by way of becoming the outstanding nympholept of the downtown metropolitan area.

A slim purse, however, pretty well circumscribed our social life, and our leisure was usually spent at home reading. Montague, employed on a garment-trade newspaper, dreamed of one day blossoming into a writer of pulp fiction. Consequently, he made a point of keeping abreast of *Argosy, Flynn's, Cupid's Diary, Railroad Stories,* and similar periodicals — solely to study their plot techniques, he was quick to assure you, for he professed to scorn their sleazy, infantile philosophy. Sprawled in a rump-sprung Morris chair, his forehead contorted in a scowl of concentration, Montague nightly applied himself to the incredible villainies and *galanteries* of the pulps. Some cut-rate leech having told him shortly before that he was anemic, my roommate was also valiantly attempting to restore his tissue tone. In the course of his evening's homework, he would work his way through a pint container of vanilla ice cream and a box of graham crackers, eating with a deliberate, maddening obduracy that in time began to take its toll of my nerves. I used to loll across the room from him on a Roman day bed covered in monk's cloth, struggling to fix my mind on the novel I was reading, but sooner or later I would detect myself staring at him in fascinated revulsion. He ate the ice cream with the small, flat wooden paddle supplied by the drugstore, sluggishly scooping up a gob, placing the paddle on his tongue, and allowing the cream to disintegrate, his slightly bovine eyes never straying from the printed page. This grisly ritual, varied only by an occasional tangerine, whose stringy rind he braided into a torque and left in the ashtray, eventually became a fixation with me. Each time he raised the paddle to his lips, I could almost taste its dry, grainy surface myself; beads of sweat the size of Malaga grapes stood forth on my brow and I ground my nails into my palms to keep from crying out. At last, the floodgates gave way. One night, I leaped to my feet, cut loose with a falsetto paraphrase of *Hedda Gabler,* and ran screaming down Macdougal Street. The next day, I moved into a single bedroom at the West Side Y.M.C.A.

I hardly expected that bittersweet epoch to return with such poignancy when, a few days ago, I picked Gertrude Atherton's *Black Oxen* out of a second-hand bin on Fourth Avenue. Then, as I thumbed through it, with the Cyclops eye of the bookseller behind the plate glass challenging me to steal it, I remembered it as the great novel of my *fin-de-siècle* period. For one freezing instant, I was propelled backward in time to my spavined day bed, torn between Mrs. Atherton's glandular *Spielerei* and Montague's odious paddle. Every dictate of good sense warned me that the prudent course would be to let the past bury its dead, flee to a Turkish bath, and go on a brannigan, but did I do it? Ah, no — I had to buy the book yet.

Black Oxen, published in 1923, achieved thirteen editions in nine months, disrupted bridge luncheons and dinner parties the country over, made its author one of the most talked-of women of the century, and brought to movie stardom a lady who, after twenty-five years, is still my dream boat. To those who remember Corinne Griffith as the Countess Marie Zattiany in the film version, I need say no more; if any gentlemen are minded to form a club like the Junta in *Zuleika Dobson,* dedicated to celebrating her sempiternal loveliness, I place at their disposal my rooms at the Albany. Rereading *Black Oxen* today, I find it difficult to be objective. I cannot altogether divorce the incomparable luster of Miss Griffith's eyes, her porcelain fragility, from the heroine of the novel, and if I should occasionally whinny or *segue* into the opening bars of "Yearning," I trust it will be taken in good part.

Ponce de León's fountain has always found favor with the popular imagination, and in choosing its modern counterpart, gland rejuvenation, as her theme, Mrs. Atherton was a sly mongoose. Her tale begins at a fashionable first night, at which we are introduced to Lee Clavering, top-flight columnist and former dramatic critic. Clavering is a schoolgirl's dream, an alloy of Heathcliff, Conrad Veidt, and Jinx Falkenburg's brother. He is thirty-four, has a long, lounging body, a dark, saturnine face, and steel-blue eyes, and, to list but four of the labels used to tag him, is fastidious, cynical, morose, and mysterious. It is superfluous to add (though the author does, and at length) that he is a thoroughgoing misogynist. Well, Mac, you must be intuitive. As the first act draws to a close, he spies in front of him a head of hair "the color of warm ashes" and "no more than a glimpse of a white neck and a suggestion of sloping shoulders." "Rather rare those, nowadays," observes Clavering to himself — a sentiment I found baffling, for most heads I recall in the twenties were part of a set that included neck and shoulders. A few minutes later, during the intermission, their owner rises and coolly scrutinizes the audience through her opera glasses. Space precludes my tabulating the niceties of her face and figure, but I may assure the reader that she's a dilly. She wears a dress of white jet, long white gloves, and a triple string of pearls whose radiance is dimmed by her eyes: "They were very dark gray eyes, Greek in the curve of the lid, and inconceivably wise, cold, disillusioned." The problem is posed; the players attend. White captures Black in an unspecified number of moves, and damn'd be he that first cries, "Hold, enough."

Once started, the plot of *Black Oxen* picks up speed like a ruptured toboggan. In the theater lobby, Clavering runs into Charles Dinwiddie, an elderly clubman and a relative of his, who likewise has been struck all of a heap, but for quite another reason. "Thirty-odd years ago," he informs Clavering, "any one of us old chaps would have told you she was Mary Ogden, and like as not raised his hat. She was the beauty and belle of her day. But she married a Hungarian diplomat, Count Zattiany, when she was twenty-four, and deserted us." Before long, the lady begins exciting popular attention as well; society and the press boil with speculation and rumor about her identity. It is pertinent to note here what a flattering level of literacy Mrs. Atherton ascribes to the journalism of the Jazz Age: "The columnists had commented on her. One had indited ten lines of free verse in her honor, another had soared on the wings of seventeenth-century English into a panegyric on her beauty and her halo of mystery. A poet-editor-wit had cleped her 'The Silent Drama.' " The last verb, incidentally, is a fair sample of Mrs. Atherton's relish for the recherché, or uptown, word. She speaks elsewhere of a "rubescent Socialist," "rhinocerene hides," and a "debauched gerontic virgin."

Despite concerted efforts of Dinwiddie and Mrs. Oglethorpe, a dowager who grew up with Mary Ogden, to probe the mystery surrounding the fair stranger, she remains a fascinating enigma. She turns up at every first night, fanning Clavering's infatuation to white heat as the weeks pass. "She never rose in her seat again, and, indeed, seemed to seek inconspicuousness, but she was always in the second or third row of the orchestra, and she wore a different gown on each occasion." A rather ineffectual method of shunning the limelight, if I may say so; it would probably have caused less comment if she had worn a fringed lampshade on her head, and a pair of snowshoes. Finally, Clavering follows her one evening to her mansion on Murray Hill. To his elation, she is not unaware of his interest. "Oh, it is you," she says with a faint smile. "I forgot my key and I cannot make anyone hear the bell. The servants sleep on the top floor, and of course like logs." Her cavalier obligingly kicks in a windowpane, and she rewards him with sandwiches and whiskey in the library, where a log is burning on the hearth — presumably some servant incapable of reaching the top floor. Out of this session comes her declaration that she is yet another Countess Zattiany, a third cousin of Mary Ogden, who, she says, is in a Vienna sanitarium. Clavering is so enamored of her Old World charm, whatever her identity, that, on reaching the sidewalk, he stands guard over the house for two hours. The heroes of current fiction exhibit such constancy all too seldom.

In a dozen hardboiled novels I could name, girls have lavished lots more than sandwiches and whiskey without any token of devotion beyond a glancing peck on the cheek.

As the story progresses and Clavering lays siege to the countess, it grows rapidly apparent that she is a *femme du monde* of vast experience for a person in her early thirties, one who has enjoyed social triumphs and knows them to be illusory. "Luncheons! Dinners! Balls! I was surfeited before the war," she observes scornfully on being pressed to re-enter society. When Clavering admiringly remarks that she must have distinguished herself abroad, she assents with fetching candor: "Oh, yes. Once an entire house — it was at the opera — rose as I entered my box at the end of the first act." Besides betraying an intimate knowledge of three decades of European diplomacy, Mme. Zattiany also drops several casual hints about Dr. Steinach, the noted Viennese endocrinologist, which should tip her mitt to the least observant, but her beau grimly refuses to tumble. For a columnist-critic represented as a blend of Jimmie Fidler and James Gibbons Huneker, Clavering is wondrously obtuse. He bumbles around with no suspicion that he has pinned his affections on a miracle of surgery, attributing her witchery to everything but the obvious medical reason. One evening, for example, they are dining at her home. "She was eating her oysters daintily and giving him the benefit of her dark brown eyelashes," states the narrative, breeding envy in those of us who have trouble gracefully manipulating our lashes, let alone our oysters. This inexplicably provokes from Clavering a genealogical litany establishing Mme. Zattiany as a Nordic princess. "Oh, yes, you are a case of atavism, no doubt," he assures her. "I can see you sweeping northward over the steppes of Russia as the ice-caps retreated . . . re-embodied on the Baltic coast or the shores of the North Sea . . . sleeping for ages in one of the Megaliths, to rise again a daughter of the Brythons, or of a Norse Viking . . . west into Anglia to appear once more as a Priestess of the Druids chaunting in a sacred grove . . . or as Boadicea — who knows!"

The upshot of these dithyrambs is, of course, a proposal of mar-   **99** riage, which ultimately compels the countess to publicly divulge her secret; namely, that she is the true Countess Zattiany (née Mary Ogden), that she is crowding fifty-eight, and that her pristine zip has been rekindled at Professor Steinach's gland parlors in Vienna. Clavering's ardor abates temporarily; he undergoes a phase of irresolution and soul-searching wherein his work suffers, but he gamely meets his obligations: "He avoided the office and wrote his column at home. Luckily a favorite old comedian had died recently. He could fill up with reminiscence and anecdote." Providential indeed, and a striking demonstration of the truth of a pair of old adages about silver linings and ill winds. At any rate, love vanquishes his misgivings, and, proposing again to the countess, who by now is a national sensation comparable to the flying saucers, he is accepted. Just as the blissful couple are making plans for a honeymoon at a shoe box in the Dolomites (it may have been a shooting box; frankly, I had no time for technicalities at this advanced stage of the story), the third leg of the triangle comes into view. Prince Moritz Franz Ernest Felix von Hohenhauer, an elder statesman of the Austrian Empire and former lover of the *Gräfin,* arrives in New York on business of state. He pursues his ex-sweetheart to a bohemian retreat in the Adirondacks, to which Clavering has spirited her, and, in the following majestic mouthful, tries to dissuade her from the marriage: "Your revivified glands have restored to you the appearance and the strength of youth, but although you have played with a role that appealed to your vanity, to your histrionic powers — with yourself as chief audience — your natural desire to see if you could not be — to yourself, again — as young as you appear, you have no more illusion in your soul than when you were a withered old woman in Vienna." Whether by his logic or by his tortured grammar, the Prince succeeds in casting a blight on the romance, and the book closes on a lovers' renunciation in Central Park as sweet as any *Linzer Torte* in Rumpelmayer's. Or, should I say, as any wooden paddleful of vanilla ice cream slowly dissolving on the tongue.

100   If my sentimental return to *Black Oxen* had any aftermath other

Black Oxen *by Gertrude Atherton*

than biliousness, it reminded me how negligent I have been of late toward my ductless glands. The last time I visited Los Angeles, there was a shop on South Figueroa in whose window was a mound of assorted jelly beans marked "Fancy male hormones and pep glands — $1.49 the pound." My next trip through, I figure to latch onto a little bag of those — say, ten cents' worth. So if you see a middle-aged chap with a dark, saturnine face, fastidious and morose, swinging around the shelves of your second-hand bookshop and chattering like a gibbon, you'll know who it is. But don't think you've got a Chinaman's chance, girls. His heart's still pledged to Corinne Griffith.

Great Aches from Little Boudoirs Grow

WHENEVER I STRETCH OUT before my incinerator, churchwarden in hand, and, staring reflectively into the dying embers, take inventory of my mottled past, I inevitably hark back to a period, in the spring of 1926, that in many ways was the most romantic of my life. I was, in that turbulent and frisky epoch, an artist of sorts, specializing in neo-primitive woodcuts of a heavily waggish nature that appeared with chilling infrequency in a moribund comic magazine. It was a hard dollar, but it allowed me to stay in bed until noon, and I was able to get by with half as many haircuts as my conventional friends above Fourteenth Street. My atelier was a second-floor rear bedroom in a handsome mansion on West Ninth Street, temporarily let out to respectable bachelors during the owner's absence abroad. In this sunny and reposeful chamber, I had set up my modest possessions: the draftsman's table and tools of my trade; a rack of costly Dunhills I never smoked; and a lamp made of a gigantic bottle, formerly an acid carboy, and trimmed with an opaque parchment shade that effectively blanketed any light it gave. After pinning up a fast batik or two, I lent further tone to the premises by shrouding the ceiling fixture with one of those prickly, polyhedral glass lampshades esteemed in the Village, a lethal contraption that was forever gouging furrows in my scalp. It met its Waterloo the evening a young person from the *Garrick Gaieties*, in a corybantic mood, swung into a cancan and executed a kick worthy of La Goulue. The crash is said to have been audible in Romany Marie's, six blocks away.

I had not been installed in my diggings very long before I found that they were not ideally suited to provide the tranquillity I had hoped for. My windows overlooked a refuge for unwed mothers operated by the Florence Crittenton League, and almost every morning between four and six the wail of newborn infants reverberated from the chimney pots. Occasionally, of an afternoon, I beheld one of the ill-starred girls on the roof, scowling at me in what I interpreted as an accusatory manner, and although I had in no way contributed to her downfall, I was forced to draw the blinds before I could regain a measure of composure. Far more disturbing, however, was the behavior of the clientele attracted by the tenant of the studio above mine, a fashionable Austrian portrait painter. This worthy, a fraudulent dauber who had parlayed an aptitude for copying Boldini and Philip de László into an income of six figures, was the current *Wunderkind* of Park Avenue; the socially prominent streamed to his dais like pilgrims to the Kaaba in Mecca. The curb in front of the house was always choked with sleek, custom-built Panhards and Fiats, and hordes of ravishing ladies, enveloped in sables and redolent of patchouli, ceaselessly surged past my door. What with the squeals and giggles that floated down from the upper landing, the smack of garters playfully snapped, and pretty objurgations stifled by kisses, I was in such a constant state of cacoëthes that I shrank to welterweight in a fortnight.

It would be unfair, though, to hold the painter entirely culpable for my condition; a good share of it was caused by a novel I was bewitched with at the time — Maxwell Bodenheim's *Replenishing Jessica*. Its publication, it will be recalled, aroused a major scandal hardly surpassed by *Lady Chatterley's Lover*. Determined efforts were made to suppress it, and it eventually gave rise to Jimmy Walker's celebrated dictum that no girl has ever been seduced by a book. Whether the *mot* was confirmed by medical testimony, I cannot remember, but in one immature reader, at least, *Replenishing Jessica* created all the symptoms of breakbone fever. So much so, in fact, that prior to a nostalgic reunion with it several days ago, I fortified myself with a half grain of codeine. I need not have bothered. Time, the great analgesic, had forestalled me.

To call the pattern of Mr. Bodenheim's story simple would be like referring to St. Peter's as roomy or Lake Huron as moist; "elementary" sums it up rather more succinctly. Condensed to its essence, *Replenishing Jessica* is an odyssey of the bedtime hazards of a young lady of fashion bent on exploring her potentialities. Jessica Maringold is the twenty-three-year-old daughter of a real-estate millionaire, willful, perverse, alternately racked by an impulse to bundle and a hankering for the arts. Without any tedious preliminaries, she weighs in on the very first page perched on a piano bench near a stockbroker named Theodore Purrel, for whom she is playing "one of Satie's light affairs." "She was a little above medium height, with a body that was quite plump between the hips and upper thighs," the author recounts, exhibiting a gusto for anatomical detail that often threatens to swamp his narrative. Purrel receives a similarly severe appraisal: "He was a tall man, just above thirty years, and he had the body of an athlete beginning to deteriorate — the first sign of a paunch and too much fat on his legs." With all this lard in proximity, it is preordained that high jinks will ensue, and they do — cataclysmically. "His fingers enveloped the fullness of her breasts quite as a boy grasps soap-bubbles and marvels at their intact resistance." The soap bubbles I grasped as a boy were not distinguished for their elasticity, but they may have been more resilient in Mr. Bodenheim's youth. Meanwhile, during these gymnastics Jessica surrenders herself to typically girlish musings. "She remembered the one night in which she had given herself to him. . . . She knew that Purrel would grasp her, and she reflected on some way of merrily repulsing him, such as pulling his tie, wrenching

Replenishing Jessica *by Maxwell Bodenheim*

his nose, tickling his ears." Unluckily, the delaying action had been futile, and Purrel managed to exact his tribute. Now, however, he impresses her as a dull, self-confident libertine, an estimate borne out by his Philistine rejection of her intellect: "I wish you'd give this mind stuff a rest. . . . It doesn't take much brains to smear a little paint on canvas and knock around with a bunch of long-haired mutts. . . . I may not be a world-beater but I've run up a fat bank account in the last eight years and you can't do *that* on an empty head." The struggle between Theodore's animal appeal and Jessica's spiritual nature is resolved fortuitously. "The frame of the piano, below the keys, was pressing into her lower spine, like an absurd remonstrance that made her mood prosaic in the passing of a second," Bodenheim explains, adding with magisterial portentousness, "The greatest love can be turned in a thrice [*sic*] to the silliest of frauds by a breaking chair, or the prolonged creaking of a couch." When the lust has blown away, Jessica is safe in her bedroom and her admirer presumably on his way to a cold shower. "Purrel felt feverish and thwarted without knowing why," says the text, though any reasonably alert chimpanzee of three could have furnished him a working hypothesis.

Jessica's next sexual skirmish takes place at twilight the following afternoon, in the studio of Kurt Salburg, a dour Alsatian painter who addresses her as "*Liebchen*" and subjects her virtue, or what's left of it, to a coarse, Teutonic onslaught. His brutal importunities, unaccompanied by the slightest appeal to her soul, provoke her into withholding her favors, but she confers them a scant twenty-four hours later on Sydney Levine, a masterful criminal lawyer, who requisitions them in the terse, direct fashion of an Army quartermaster ordering sixty bags of mule feed. "I have wanted you for six months," Levine tells her. "I have no lies or romantic pretenses to give you. My love for you is entirely physical, and nothing except complete possession will satisfy it. . . . From now on, it would be impossible to control myself in your presence, and it will have to be everything or nothing." Their romp leaves Jessica remorseful and more frustrated than ever. Eschewing the opposite sex for three weeks, she stays glued to her easel, creating futuristic pictures apropos of which the author observes, "She had a moderate talent for painting." The sample he describes would appear to permit some room for discussion: ". . . two lavender pineapples, placed on each side of a slender, black and white vase, all of the articles standing on a dark red table that seemed about to fall on the cerise floor." Of course, there is always the possibility that Mr. Bodenheim is being sardonic, just as there is always the possibility that the Princess Igor Troubetzkoy is planning to leave me her stock in the five-and-ten-cent stores.

Ostensibly purified by her joust with the Muse, Jessica now retreads her steps to Salburg's studio to bedevil him a bit further. This time the lecherous Alsatian uses a more devious gambit to achieve his ends. He employs the infantile, or blubber-mouth, approach. " 'If

you should refuse me now, I would never live again,' he said, in a low
voice. 'Never, never . . . I am helpless and frightened, Jessica.' His
words had a defenceless quiver that could not be disbelieved. . . .
A disrobed and frantic boy was speaking his fear that she might whip
his naked breast." Following a rough-and-tumble interlude, the par-
ticipants spend the evening at a *Nachtlokal* with Purrel, whom Jessica
pits against Salburg to keep things humming. In the resulting scrim-
mage, the stockbroker draws first claret; Jessica is repelled by the
artist's craven behavior and, dismissing her flames as bullies and
cowards, decides to pop over to Europe and see what beaux are avail-
able in England. There is a vignette of her, aboard ship, calculated
to awake tender memories in the older girls: "She was dressed in dark
purple organdy with white rosettes at the waist, stockings and shoes
of the same purple hue, a long, thin cape of white velvet, and a pale
straw turban trimmed with black satin." It is a coincidence worth recording that the young person from the *Garrick Gaieties* referred to
earlier wore exactly this costume when she danced the cancan in my
web. Naturally, she removed the long, thin cape of white velvet to
facilitate her kick at the lamp, but in every other respect her en-
semble was identical. Sort of spooky, when you come to think of it.

Having installed herself in an apartment in Chelsea, Jessica plunges
intrepidly into the bohemian whirl of London, keeping a weather
eye out for brainy males. At the 1919 Club, a rendezvous so named
"in commemoration of a Russian revolution" — an aside that pricks
your curiosity as to which one the author means — she encounters
four. They are (disguised under impenetrable pseudonyms) Ramsay
MacDonald, the Sitwell brothers, and Aldous Huxley, but, regrettable
to say, no pyrotechnics of note occur. At last, the situation brightens.
One evening, Jessica finds herself in her flat discussing Havelock Ellis
with a personable ex-officer named Robert Chamberlain, ". . . and
during the course of the talk Jessica partly unloosened her heliotrope
blouse because of the warmness of the room, and sprawled at ease
on a couch without a thought of sensual invitation." Innocent as the
gesture is, Chamberlain in his crass, masculine way misconstrues it.   *107*

"His confidently thoughtful mood was shattered, and for the first time he looked steadily at the tapering, disciplined curve of her legs, slowly losing their plumpness as their lines fell to her ankles, and half revealed by her raised, white skirt; and the sloping narrowness of her shoulders, and her small-lipped, impishly not quite round face that was glinting and tenuous in the moderated light of the room." But the foregoing is merely a feint on Bodenheim's part, and two months of interminable palaver are necessary before his creatures coalesce to make great music. The slow buildup plainly does much to intensify Chamberlain's fervor: "His mind changed to a fire that burned without glowing — a black heat — and his emotions were dervishes." Once the pair wind up in the percale division, the same old sense of disillusion begins gnawing at Jessica. A week of stormy bliss and she is off to New York again, hastily sandwiching in a last-minute affair with Joseph Israel, a London real-estate broker.

The concluding fifty pages of *Replenishing Jessica* cover a span of approximately six years and vibrate with the tension of high-speed oatmeal. Jessica passes through a succession of lovers (including poets, musical-comedy stars, and other migratory workers), marries and discards Purrel, and inherits four million dollars, zestfully described as composed of real estate, bonds, and cash. (Offhand, I cannot recall another novel in which the scarlet threads of sex and real estate are so inextricably interwoven. It's like a union of Fanny Hill and Bing & Bing.) All these stimulating experiences, nevertheless, are no more than "a few snatchings at stars that turned out to be cloth ones sewed to the blue top of a circus tent," though one suspects a handful of the spangles may have been negotiable. Tired of drifting about the capitals of Europe and unable to find a mate who offers the ideal blend of sensuality and savvy, she devotes herself to teaching children to paint at an East Side settlement house. Here, among the lavender pineapples she is midwifing, she meets a saintly, partially deformed type given to reading Flaubert and writing aesthetic critiques. His luxuriant brown beard, exalted eyes, and general Dostoevskian halo augur well, and as the flyleaves loom, Jessica's saga ends with an elegiac quaver reminiscent of a Jesse Crawford organ solo.

Every book of consequence ultimately produces lesser works that bear its influence, and *Replenishing Jessica* is no exception. As collateral reading, I can recommend a small semi-scientific monograph I myself recently helped to prepare. It concerns itself with the peculiar interaction of codeine and ennui on a white hysteroid male of forty-four exposed to a bookful of erotic fancies. Unlike the average hypnotic subject, the central character was fully conscious at all times, even while asleep. He ate a banana, flung the skin out of the window, flung the book after the skin, and was with difficulty restrained from following. It sounds technical but it really isn't. It's an absorbing document, and above all it's as clean as a whistle. Not a single bit of smooching in it from start to finish. I made certain of *that*.

Mayfair Mama, Turn Your Damper Down

THE second-class-passenger complement of the S. S. *Leviathan,* eastbound for Cherbourg in June, 1927, included some rare birds. There was an opulent Frenchwoman of a certain age on whom Toulouse-Lautrec had reputedly squandered his patrimony, a Belgian bicycle team fresh from the six-day races at the Garden, an elderly dandy of the era of Berry Wall who claimed to have had more than a waltzing acquaintance with the Jersey Lily, and a Greek gem dealer with a black monocle and a Malacca stick containing a handful of uncut diamonds. At least, he *said* they were diamonds, and I, dizzied by my first trip abroad and saturated with Maurice Dekobra's *The Madonna of the Sleeping Cars,* joyously accepted his confidence. I doubt whether anyone else so rabid for adventure has ever embarked on a maiden voyage to Europe. I was ready for every contingency — international cardsharps, dacoits, and, particularly, veiled charmers with mocking mouths who might entice me to Salonika. Folded at the bottom of my suitcase, where they could be easily stolen, were blueprints of a mitrailleuse I had cooked up, together with a trench coat suitable for tracking the culprits through the purlieus of Stambul. I sat in the smoking lounge of the ocean greyhound expelling thin jets of Turkish from my nostrils until my head rang like a burglar alarm. I cultivated a hooded, watchful gaze.

Contrary to the hopes inspired by Dekobra's novel, almost nothing happened to me on the crossing, and when it did, it was of a completely unexpected nature. The second day out, a gusty, obstreperous party named Lightfoot was moved into my cabin. He was a man of shattering vitality, a combination of Olsen and Johnson, with an explosive guffaw that set the lifeboats quivering in their davits. A compulsive talker in the great tradition, Lightfoot instantly peppered me with his history and aspirations, downing a hogshead of bourbon meanwhile. He had been a World War ace, he told me, and was currently en route to Le Bourget, from which he proposed to fly the Atlantic solo. He predicted that this would overshadow Lindy's feat, and I agreed unequivocally, since he made no mention of using an airplane for the hop.

Time has mercifully dimmed the memory of our association during the next five days, but one episode remains untarnished. Lightfoot and I occupied a table in the dining saloon with a mousy schoolteacher from South Braintree — a Miss Purvis — and a fattish, mealy androgyne called Rossiter, who was going to the Hook of Holland to study counterpoint. Lightfoot promptly dedicated himself to making Rossiter's life a burden. He lay awake nights contriving practical jokes to play on the musician, each more barbarous than the last. They reached their climax one noon when Rossiter was late for luncheon. Adjuring us to secrecy, Lightfoot produced a baking-powder biscuit of sponge rubber, one of those realistic facsimiles sold in magic-supply shops. I presume it was part of his traveling kit, for, well equipped as the *Leviathan* was, it carried no gear of that kind. He then smothered it in sauce, dabbed sauce on our three plates for authenticity, and gleefully awaited Rossiter. The latter, his appetite sharpened by a turn around the deck, sat down and addressed the

The Madonna of the Sleeping
Cars *by Maurice Dekobra*

hors-d'œuvre with relish. As his fork pressed into the biscuit, it discharged a mournful squeal that short-circuited conversation all over the room. People half rose, craning their necks and peering spellbound at Rossiter. Apparently unable to credit his ears, he again cut into the biscuit, and again the hidden mechanism responded. In the attendant wave of mirth, cued by Lightfoot's bellow, Rossiter stood up with simple dignity and, I am glad to report, flung the delicacy into his tormentor's face.

The acquisitive instinct dies hard. Pawing over the detritus in my bookshelf latterly, I was confronted after two decades with the very copy of *The Madonna of the Sleeping Cars* that had set me roving. Unlike its owner, its spine was still erect and soldierly and its jacket free of mildew. The temptation to see what sort of tinsel had capti-vated me at twenty-three, as well as to spend a couple of hours on my shoulder blades, was irresistible. Before you could say Maurice Deko-bra, I was in the horizontal, drinking in the stuff in great, thirsty gulps.

The tale M. Dekobra told so artfully that it tore through five edi-tions like a sickle-bar mower was, between ourselves, no trail blazer. The formula of high life and low loins, to borrow Aldous Huxley's apposite phrase, had long been employed by E. Phillips Oppenheim, Paul Morand, and other writers of that genre. Dekobra merely souped it up, adding a high-octane element few novelists had taken advan-tage of until then — Soviet Russia. There may have been earlier vari-ations on the theme of the Beauty and the Bolshevik, but I venture that there had been none more foolish.

The title of *The Madonna of the Sleeping Cars* prefigures its ex-otic and shifting locale; the narrative, related by a singular coxcomb named Prince Séliman, veers from London to Berlin, from Vienna to the Caucasus, and from Monaco to Loch Lomond with a breathless-ness unmatched outside a *Vogue* fashion forecast. The Prince, a Frenchman whose patent to nobility is never made quite clear, is at the outset footloose in London, recently separated from his wealthy American wife. An advertisement in the personal column of the *Times* secures him a position as private secretary to a lovely gadabout widow called Lady Diana Wynham. "In Paris," observes Dekobra as he pro-ceeds to describe her high cheekbones, sensual lips, and limpid eyes, "there is a saying that when an Englishwoman is beautiful she is very beautiful." Trust the French to coin a nifty like that; no wonder they produced Voltaire. At any rate, the comely peeress has earned an international reputation for audacity and chic. She shyly confesses that "there is not a customs officer in any country who doesn't recog-nize the perfume of my valises, and who doesn't know the most sacred details of my lingerie." Having spent the better part of two million pounds since her husband's death, she feels she needs a cool head to counsel her, and offers Prince Séliman five hundred pounds a month to do so. He takes the post but spurns the money, declaring he wishes only relief from boredom: "I don't rent my services, I give them." At twenty-three, I understood his motives perfectly; I had done the same kind of thing on innumerable occasions. Today, I incline to sleep on it.

One of the Prince's first assignments is to conduct Lady Diana to a session with a celebrated psychologist, Professor Siegfried Traurig, to have a dream of hers interpreted. The reader gets a foretaste here of Dekrobra's love of the salty simile, a passion that is to boil over later, when he speaks of "those European clinics where they dig up the soul with the shovel of introspection and where they slice apart the elements of the will with the chisel of psychopathic analysis." Equally poetic figures are evoked, farther on, by a description of a caviar binge ("As the lemon wept acid tears on the delicacy, etc.") and by Lady Diana's treatment of a lover ("I . . . put my guest under the cold shower-bath of refusal and then on the burning flame of hope"). Subsequently, in a petulant mood, she excoriates the Prince for his horrid logic, "which inevitably throws the wild horses of imagination with its lasso." It is significant that once the steeds start bucking, Dekobra himself conveniently mislays that old riata.

To continue: Professor Traurig elicits the details of Lady Diana's dream, orders the Prince to kiss her, and photographs what is represented to be a spectral analysis of her reactions — standard psychoanalytical technique, as any fool knows. The basic test reveals that she has a perfection neurosis, which one presumes will yield to a little snake oil, and our heroine blithely goes her way. The plot now starts bubbling in the percolator. Rumor spreads that Sumatra-rubber stocks, her ladyship's chief investment, are shaky, and tradespeople begin to dun her. Seeking to divert their attention momentarily, Lady Diana causes a scandal, by executing a shocking dance at a charity matinée. Her costume will be helpful to those in a tight financial spot. It consists of "a *cache-sexe* no bigger than the hand of a sacristan and held in place by an almost invisible garland of bindweed, two buskins with silver ribbons, and a veil of white mousseline which hung down to her elbows." Of course, if you live in an area where sacristans and bindweed are unobtainable, you will simply have to improvise, but anybody with an ounce of initiative can make do.

The chandeliers have hardly ceased rocking before Lady Diana has another brainstorm. Fifteen thousand acres of oil lands near Telav, on the Black Sea, formerly owned by her hubby, have been nationalized by the Bolsheviks. However, she has information that the Soviet delegate to Berlin, Leonid Varichkine, can be bribed into allowing her to exploit them. Prince Séliman departs forthwith to brace him. At the Walhalla Restaurant, in Bellevuestrasse, he and Varichkine, a smooth apple in Bond Street clothes, get together over half a dozen 1911 Heidsieck Monopole. The Russian knows what he wants, and it isn't petroleum: "I'll countersign the papers for her concession when the rising sun surprises her in my arms." In the higher echelons, obviously, proposals of the sort are a commonplace; Séliman, unruffled, wires his principal, and she arrives to look Varichkine over. In the meantime, another, and sinister, character has entered the wings — Mme. Irina Mouravieff, the delegate's mistress and herself a power with the Politburo. She tacks up a "No Poaching" sign, accompanied by dire threats. Everybody, naturally, ignores her caveat; and understandably, because otherwise the chlorophyll would drain out of the story. Varichkine, in fact, is so smitten with Lady Diana that he offers his hand, and she, attracted by the uproar the marriage would excite in Berkeley Square, accepts it. The round ends with Mme. Mouravieff darkly promising the Prince, who she feels is in some way culpable, that he will rue the day. He counters with an epigram, shaped like a cheese blintz, to the effect that "a man who is warned is worth two ordinary men." As events prove, he would have done better to stow the bravado and tighten up his accident policy.

Reduced to essentials, the rest of the yarn treats of Mme. Mouravieff's revenge. She lures the Prince to Nikolaïa, in the Caucasus, to inspect the oil lands, by trailing before him a cuddly *Mädchen* named Klara, with a mutinous nose and a mole on her cheekbone. Séliman and Klara flirt their way into the swansdown in Vienna, and in Constantinople, weakened by raisins, she acknowledges being a Russian agent and warns him to turn back. He takes ship for Batum nevertheless, and at Trebizond encounters another obstacle — his wife, Griselda, cruising aboard her yacht with friends. They exchange sighs over bygone ecstasies, seem about to become reconciled, and then hearken to the plot, which beckons the Prince on to Muscovy. Shortly after he reaches Nikolaïa, the trap is sprung, and he lands in an underground cell operated by the Cheka.

The idiom thereafter, up to the time the Prince escapes on his wife's yacht, has been made tolerably familiar by such savants as Eugene Lyons and George Sokolsky. I shall not queer their pitch beyond saying that Dekobra, too, is a pretty deft man with a Red atrocity. Mme. Mouravieff is, of course, on hand at all hours to chivy and gloat, but the Prince finally slips his leash. Off the Riviera, he and his wife adjust their differences, a minor climax preceding a whirl-wind finish at Castle Glensloy, in Scotland. Here the jealous Russky hunts down Lady Diana ("Two tigresses facing one another. The daughter of the Mongols against the daughter of the Celts. Two races. Two worlds. . . . Above all, two women"), draws a heater on her rival, and is pistoled by Varichkine. The curtain rings down on Milady bidding adieu to her devoted secretary at the Gare de l'Est as the Orient Express snorts impatiently in the background. She has brushed off Varichkine and is faring forth in quest of someone "who will cater to my whims and ripen in my safe-deposit box some golden apples from the garden of Hesperides." Which, let us fervently hope, she will pare with the platinum fruit knife of restraint.

No doubt my senses were sharpened razor-keen by contact with the world of intrigue and counterplot, because just as I closed *The Madonna of the Sleeping Cars* I detected a soft footfall outside my room and the sound of the doorknob being tried gently. In a flash, I realized that it was my family, come to spy on my movements. Quick as a cat, I popped the book into my jumper, removed my teeth, and pretended to be deep in slumber when they entered. It was a close shave, for had they caught me, I would have had short shrift. This way, I have not only long shrift but Dekobra — and, baby, that's enough to make anybody's cup run over.

Stringing up Father

PARDON ME, friend, would you happen to know the technical term for a man who walks around for three days with a
letter in his pocket he's afraid to mail? Not a blackmail note, a
billet-doux, or a plea for a small loan — nothing like that; a perfectly
straightforward letter to a publisher containing a coupon and my
check for five dollars. Ever since Sunday, I've been screwing up courage to drop it into a postbox, but I just can't bring it off. The thing is,
if I temporize any longer, my son isn't going to have a copy of *The
Life Stories of America's 50 Foremost Business Leaders* for his birthday, and that would be calamitous. Or would it? God, I wish I knew.

What pitchforked me into this imbroglio was a full-page advertisement for the work in the New York *Times* "Book Review," bordered
with photographs of the fifty industrialists reputed to control our
destiny. At first glance, I mistook them for trophies used to illustrate
some book like Jim Corbett's *Man-Eaters of Kumaon*, but on closer
examination I saw that their heads were much smaller than the average Bengal tiger's, and that a few of them, including Henry Luce and
David Sarnoff, looked surprisingly benign. "What intriguing quirks
of fate swayed the early careers of these men?" the text asked, but-
tonholing me and exuding an opulent aroma of Drambuie and Corona
Coronas. "You'll be amazed by these revealing life stories, telling how
the 50 foremost business leaders in the country sensed their oppor-
tunities and made the most of them! . . . An ideal book for distribu-
tion to executives. Or the perfect gift from father to son." The final
sentence brought me into camp. I had been casting about for some

useful remembrance for a twelve-year-old who already has more chemistry kits, cyclotrons, and disintegrators than you can shake a fist at, and it struck me that here was the ideal present — romantic but factual, pragmatic, shrewdly designed to stimulate youthful incentive. Crowing with self-satisfaction at my acumen, I filled out the necessary details and, sealing them in an envelope, leisurely resumed reading the advertisement.

My *amour-propre* deserted me abruptly when I reached a paragraph indicating how one of our most noted tycoons got his start. It was the account of his preternatural initiative that pinned back my ears and begot an odd, gnawing squeamishness about putting *The Life Stories of America's 50 Foremost Business Leaders* into Junior's hands. "James H. Rand," blandly read the blurb, "working under his father, suddenly hit upon the invention of a visible index. With full confidence in his abilities, he immediately launched his own business in direct competition with his father. Several years of intense and heated rivalry followed. The outcome saw the father completely bought out . . . the son well on his way to forming the giant Remington Rand of today."

It may be psychologically wholesome to prime the young with examples like the preceding, but, indulgent father though I am, I'm beginning to think that I would sooner present mine with a can of smokeless powder and a stiletto. I submit that the latent desire to make a monkey out of Daddy will flourish of its own accord, and I do not propose to lug pails of water to insure its growth. I do, nevertheless, feel it incumbent on me to elucidate the tensions implicit in such a father-and-son relationship, and, with that object, I offer in easily digestible dramatic form the case of John Prester, of the Prester John Pistol Company. Overture and incidental music, *Kapellmeister.*

> SCENE: *The office of John Prester, head of the Prester John Pistol Company, manufacturers of the celebrated Presjo Water Pistol. The roll-top desk, wall telephone, and Oliver typewriter invest the premises with an air of fusty conservatism, accentuated by the presence onstage of Millspaugh, an elderly Dickensian bookkeeper in sleeve guards and green eyeshade. As the*

curtain rises, he is staring glumly at a faded oleo that portrays a Victorian schoolboy spraying a pompous banker in silk hat and Prince Albert with a water pistol, surmounted by the legend "Presjo — Best by Test." He has turned away with a lugubrious sigh when Prester, a vigorous, hearty soul in his mid-forties, bustles in. His plump, freshly shaven face and his eyes, twinkling behind octagonal lenses, bespeak a buoyant optimism. Scaling his Homburg at a coat tree, he claps Millspaugh ebulliently on the back.

PRESTER: Morning, Millspaugh! Glorious day, what? (*Inhaling noisily.*) Gad, it's great to be alive.

MILLSPAUGH: Is it?

PRESTER: Crest of the wave, dear boy — treading on air. (*Humorously.*) How's your corporosity sagaciating?

MILLSPAUGH: It isn't.

PRESTER: Little touch of liver, eh? Thought you looked a shade regusted. Well, bear up — rise above it. We're only dead once. Ha, ha, ha.

MILLSPAUGH: Full of ginger today, aren't you?

PRESTER: Who wouldn't be? Fine fall weather, orders pouring in —

MILLSPAUGH: What makes you think so?

PRESTER (*waving toward window*): Why, all our vans rolling by, loaded with merchandise.

MILLSPAUGH: Don't you notice anything strange about them?

PRESTER (*perplexed*): No-o-o. Well, now you speak of it, they seem to be rolling in the wrong direction.

MILLSPAUGH: Precisely — right back to the warehouse.

PRESTER: You — you mean those are cancellations?

MILLSPAUGH: Chief, I don't like to upset you, but we've got the largest inventory of water pistols in the Western Hemisphere, and fresh carloads are arriving by every freight.

PRESTER: But, confound it, it's impossible — it can't be! Prester John's pioneered in squirt guns since 1889! Every red-blooded American boy —

MILLSPAUGH: Yes, yes, I've read the promotion, too. John, don't fight your custard. The public taste has changed.

PRESTER: Stuff and nonsense! Nothing'll ever replace the old-fashioned water pistol.

MILLSPAUGH (*gloomily*): Nothing but bankruptcy.

PRESTER: Damn it all, we're tops in the nuisance field! For silent, deadly accuracy, for sheer aggravation power, what other mischief-maker can touch the Presjo?

MILLSPAUGH: Well, if you must know, the Griller-Diller.

PRESTER: Pah! That toy!

MILLSPAUGH: All right, but whoever got the hunch to use muriatic acid to administer a superficial burn was a genius. It's sweeping the nation.

PRESTER: So did the exploding cigar, the dribble glass, and the hotfoot. I've seen these fads mushroom before.

MILLSPAUGH: Look, boss, just to meet the threat, couldn't we use a mild acid solution, too? Not enough to blind the victim — just give him a bad fright.

PRESTER: Now, see here, Millspaugh. Water was good enough for my father and it's good enough for me.

MILLSPAUGH: Well, then, you'd better face facts. We've got nineteen dollars in the bank. We're stony — *nettoyé* — snafu. The next voice you hear will be that of the bailiff.

PRESTER (*aghast*): What are you saying?

MILLSPAUGH: Furthermore, the president of Griller-Diller's due here any minute to buy you out, and if you want to save your skin, you'll knock under.

PRESTER: I'm not licked yet! They want a scrap, eh? I'll mortgage every penny — Thisbe can take in washing —

MILLSPAUGH: It's no good, John. He's got the whip hand.

PRESTER (*shoulders bowed*): Who is this — this upstart?

MILLSPAUGH: Nobody knows. He's sort of a mystery man, a younger Howard Hughes. He may even be the man *behind* Howard Hughes. (*There is a peremptory knock at the door, and Millspaugh exits through the window — a pretty maladroit* jeu de théâtre, *but better than having two characters carom off each other in the doorway.* **119**

Lester Prester enters. Though scarcely thirteen, his suavity and poise are immediately manifest. He wears a morning coat, bowler, and boutonnière, and rotates between his clenched teeth an unlit Havana — clearly a man accustomed to give orders and have them obeyed on the double.)

PRESTER: Oh, hello, son. Er — listen, I'm tied up — I expect a party —

LESTER: I know you do. He's here.

PRESTER *(jumping up agitatedly)*: Where? Outside?

LESTER *(with a wintry smile)*: No, inside. You're face to face with him. *(Prester's lips go ashen and he clutches the desk for support.)* Now, look, old-timer, let's have no blubbering or histrionics. You're on a lee shore and you're breaking up fast. Do you want me to throw you a li·.e or don't you?

PRESTER *(smiting his breast)*: That my own flesh and blood should spawn the Griller-Diller — no, no, I can't stand it!

LESTER *(crisply)*: Yup, we live in a changing world. Well, suppose we drop the Old Testament delivery and get down to brass tacks. I'll give you two hundred frogskins for the good will and fixtures, and I'll try to make a job for you in my shipping room. I know it's a silly, sentimental gesture and I'll live to regret it, but there it is.

PRESTER: You loathsome little scorpion. To think I dandled you on my knee.

LESTER: Relax, governor, or you'll blow a fuse. What the hell, it happens to everyone. You just got caught in the technological buzz saw, that's all.

PRESTER *(trembling)*: Where'd you get the money to float that rotten contraption? Out of my cashbox?

LESTER: No, I sold the old lady's solitaire. After all, I had to hire a public-relations counsel, didn't I?

PRESTER: What for?

LESTER *(pityingly)*: Cripes, you certainly are living in the Ice Age. Why, to start a whispering campaign about your product — to poison kids' minds against it.

"Even a roach wouldn't stab his sire in the back the way you have."

PRESTER: How — how did you do that?

LESTER: Oh, by saying it was sissy, and full of germs, and a mosquito breeder — elementary stuff. Then we got an unfrocked psychiatrist to write a paper proving it was harmful to the libido.

PRESTER: But *you* couldn't manufacture the Griller-Diller and distribute it, you little snake.

LESTER (*coolly*): Your competitor could. I just gave Twinkletoy a list of your customers in return for fifty-one per cent of the stock, we undercut your prices, and the rest was lagniappe.

PRESTER (*foundering in a bog of metaphor*): Even a roach wouldn't stab his sire in the back the way you have.

LESTER: It's business, Fatso. Dog eat dog, law of the jungle. Well, can't stand here jawing with you all day. (*He opens door, beckons in a pair of burly workmen laden with dictaphones and fluorescent lamps.*) O.K., boys, make with the brawn. Better strike that desk. I won't need it.

WORKMAN: What'll we do with the old gink?

LESTER: Tuck him in a storeroom somewhere, he's strictly non compos. (*As the workman slings Prester's inert body over his back and goes off, Lester crosses to the telephone, whips off the receiver.*) Get me Norman Bel Geddes. . . . Hello, Norman Bel? Lester Prester. Now, look, I want a desk a helicopter can land on.

CURTAIN

Methinks He Doth Protein Too Much

> SHE HAS given beauty a new category, he thought, for she appears to be edible. She is the word made fruit, rather than flesh, and with sugar and cream she would be delicious. Her neck would taste like an English apple, a pippin or nonpareil; and her arms, still faintly sunburned from the mountain snow, like greengages.—*From a short story by Eric Linklater in Harper's Bazaar.*

IN THE precise, methodical manner that characterized everything he did, Monroe Fruehauf unhurriedly read his way through the weather summary and the maritime intelligence in his morning newspaper. A low-pressure area obtained over the Laurentian Plateau, and scattered showers impended in the Carolinas. According to the list of outgoing freighters carrying mail, the *Zulu Queen* was accepting parcel post and printed matter for Lourenso Marques, Nyasaland Protectorate, Kenya, and Uganda. None of these advices occasioned Monroe surprise, or, indeed, any overwhelming concern. For all he cared, it could rain frogs over the Carolinas, and the *Zulu Queen* could carry marijuana if she were so disposed; he was merely pursuing an ingrained custom of thoroughly digesting the paper before he left for work. Not that there was any particular urgency in that respect. Nobody cared what time he opened his second-hand bookshop on West Fourth Street, and it would be hours before the first furtive schoolboy appeared in quest of the *Heptameron* or the works of Sacher-Masoch. Monroe leafed back through the paper for a final, **123** encompassing glance and discovered that he had neglected the food column. With the same tranquillity he had shown the weather and the shipping news, he learned that a new water-ground corn meal was being milled in Vermont, that an even more expensive turkey had been deviled for the millionaire palate, and that anchovies could be blended with mucilage to form an effective centerpiece for the *smörgåsbord* tray.

The last item in the column, however, definitely pricked Monroe's interest. An alert organization known as Yale Lox Associates had instituted a service to deliver a tasty assortment of smoked salmon, pot cheese, and bagels suitable for Sunday breakfast to one's door by fleet-footed, courteous messenger. A piquant notion, thought Monroe. The cooking facilities in his one-room apartment were limited, and he liked to linger abed of a Sabbath morning. The idea of having so baronial a tidbit brought to his couch was seductive. Acting on impulse, a thing he rarely did, he rang up the service forthwith. The brisk, executive voice that answered assured him that, barring a cataclysm, the lox would go through on time.

"Better throw in an extra order of rolls," said Monroe in a burst of recklessness. After all, once he had made the gesture, there was no sense stinting himself.

"Double bagels it is, sir," confirmed the voice, and Monroe almost fancied he heard heels clicked smartly. Before the day's trivia crowded the matter from his mind, he reflected pleasantly on the sybaritic experience in store. The step he had taken was hardly significant, and yet he had the inescapable feeling that he was standing on the threshold of a new life.

At eleven o'clock Sunday morning Monroe rolled over with a groan and groped about blindly for his slippers. The repeated buzz of the doorbell had settled into a long, maddening whine. Struggling into a robe, he reeled across the room, fumbled with the chain latch, and wrenched open the door. In the hallway stood a pert young woman clad in the parade uniform of a horse dragoon — giant black shako, befrogged tunic, jackboots, and sabretache depending from her belt.

As Monroe goggled at her, she raised a bugle to her lips and executed a brassy flourish that sent echoes vibrating through the stair well.

"Hey, for Pete's sake!" protested Monroe, recoiling. "You'll wake up the whole block!"

Ignoring his protest, the young woman saluted crisply and addressed him in a ringing, declamatory tone: "The Yale Lox Associates bid you good appetite. From the ice-blue waters of Newfoundland, we bring you the pink perfection of Nova Scotia salmon smoked over hickory fires; from lush upstate New York farms, loud with the hum of bees, the crumbly goodness of snowy pot cheese made of richest Jersey milk; and from the aromatic ovens of Hester Street, the lordly, succulent bagel, agleam with flavorful spar varnish. Allow me." She picked up the field kitchen at her side and brushed past Monroe into his cubicle. Dazed and unnerved by her masterful manner, he followed, feebly muttering excuses for the disordered state of the room.

"Perfectly all right. We're used to it in our work," she assured him, deftly producing a number of wax-paper packages from the container. "That the kitchenette there? Now, you just laze around. I'll have everything ready in a jiffy." She was as good as her word; by the time he emerged from the bathroom, feeling a bit less thorny, the breakfast was invitingly spread on the table, and coffee was brewing in the percolator. Impressed, Monroe inquired if these ministrations were routine.

"All part of the service." She smiled, extracted a pencil from her shako, and scribbled a bill. "Natch, if you want the comics read to you, that's a quarter extra." Not ordinarily susceptible to feminine charm, Monroe had to admit that the girl was deucedly pretty. Her cheeks had the delicate flush of a ripe peach, her ears glowed like tiny shrimps below her taffy-colored hair, and the curve of her firm, gracile hips, encased in skin-tight breeches, called to mind the rounded outlines of a prize Bartlett pear.

"Look, miss," Monroe began lamely. "Please don't misunderstand me, but I was wondering if — that is, would you share this with me, maybe?"

"Oh, I couldn't do that, sir," she said quickly. "Mr. Fabricant's rules are very strict." One of the dragoons, it seemed, had been court-martialed for just such a breach of discipline and sentenced to slice sturgeon for thirty days. So free of guile was Monroe's entreaty, though, so candid his demeanor, that at length she consented to accept a cup of coffee. Under skillful cross-questioning, she revealed that her name was Norma Ganz, that her hobbies were cooking, baking, and cleaning, that she made her own clothes (except, to be sure, those she was wearing), that she preferred symphony concerts to night clubs, and a good book to either, and that she thought most girls nowadays were extravagant, selfish, and shallow. Confronted with this paragon, Monroe's eyes glistened. Her husband, he suggested, excusing himself for the personal nature of the remark, must be a happy man indeed. Not only was she unmarried, Norma replied forlornly, but she was practically an orphan, unless one counted her father, a wealthy oil operator in Oklahoma, to whose estate she was sole legatee.

It cost Monroe a series of expensive dinners, numerous theater tickets, and over sixty dollars' worth of flowers and baubles to test the validity of Norma's story, but he eventually satisfied himself. Not one word of it was true. In addition to being an inveterate liar, Norma led a complicated dream life in which she steadfastly identified herself with the heroine of whatever movie or confession romance impressed her at the moment. She was slovenly, vain, illiterate, and altogether a source of increasing anguish to her admirer. And yet to Monroe, fully aware of her defections, she was the most toothsome morsel imaginable. His taste buds yearned for her; he could not look upon her plump white shoulders, the creamy expanse of her throat, without wanting to gobble them up as greedily as a schoolgirl might a charlotte russe. In his amorous fancy, her charms acquired a lusciousness, a dietary significance, unlike those of any other woman he had ever known. As his craving for Norma intensified, he was alarmed to find that she daily grew more disembodied; repeatedly he caught himself regarding her less as a person than a snack, a delectable

hors-d'œuvre that dominated his dreams. Sometimes, standing in his shop staring emptily at a first edition of *Jurgen* that in the past would have moved him to rapture, the thought of her succulence set his heart hammering and he groaned. Conversely, his desire for food slackened. Appreciably thinner, his eyes sunk in their sockets, he paced the streets for hours struggling to throw off his obsession, although deep down he knew the struggle to be futile. It was only a question of time, an obscure voice whispered, before the demon that bestrode him would assert itself. With a conviction of utter fatality, Monroe, drearily awaited the climax of the nightmare.

The first hint of it came several evenings later as he sat in a booth at a Brass Rail, a fork idle in his nerveless fingers and his gaze ravenously fixed on Norma. She had never looked lovelier or more esculent; it required every ounce of Monroe's self-control to prevent his hurdling the table and sinking his teeth into her rosy rind. She ate with the slow, ponderous concentration of a heifer, incapable of speech while her energies were devoted to masticating. Sated at last, she suddenly took cognizance of her escort's reverie.

"What's the matter?" she asked. "Aren't you hungry?"

"Hungry?" repeated Monroe. He uttered a harsh, melodramatic snort. "I'll say I am. I'm starving."

"Then why don't you eat your London broil?" asked Norma reasonably. "Go on, try it."

"Listen, Norma," said Monroe with low, fierce intensity, leaning forward and clasping her hand in both of his. "I've never felt this way toward any girl before."

"I *beg* your pardon," said Norma haughtily, endeavoring to disentangle herself and upsetting horseradish in the process. "I hardly think this the time or place —"

"There couldn't be a better," Monroe interrupted. "Norma — please — hear me out. I need you, I want you."

"Have you gone crazy?" Norma asked. "In a public restaurant. I ought to slap your face."

"You don't know what you do to me," pleaded Monroe, salivating as his words tumbled impetuously over one another. "You have eyes like black olives, your teeth are like pearl onions, your lips like

127

strawberry cheesecake! I could swallow you in one big gulp."

A sudden gleam of comprehension, mingled with relief, flashed over Norma's face. "Oh, is *that* all?" she said indifferently. "You mean I make you hungry."

"Has — has anyone else told you that?" asked Monroe, thunder-struck.

"*Have* they?" Norma snickered. "Practically every wolf that subscribes to the Yale Lox Associates, not to mention Mr. Fabricant."

"I thought it was just my own imagination," her swain faltered.

"Be your age," she advised maternally, squinting into her compact. "Why do you suppose I wear those cowboy gauntlets with the fringe? Some *shmendrick's* always trying to nibble on my wrists. Brother, you should see what I go through on a Sunday morning."

"But it's dangerous," objected Monroe. "You might run into a party you couldn't handle. Someone who's really — well, anthropophagous." As delicately as he could, and with guarded allusions to the Ituri Forest and the remoter tribes of Micronesia, he explained that long pig is still esteemed by primitive connoisseurs and that the likelihood of Norma's encountering similar eccentrics in her hazardous profession must not be discounted. Norma was inclined to treat his qualms airily. The most difficult situations could be resolved with a well-placed kick in the groin, she asserted, and Monroe would be the first to get one if he stepped out of line.

Looking back at this occasion afterward, in the light of the ultimate tragedy, Monroe was wont to chide himself bitterly. He should have forced the issue, compelled Norma to quit her job, had her shadowed or even kidnaped to protect her from harm. But then, he would tell himself with numb despair, how bootless to attempt to circumvent destiny; it was kismet, it had all been ordained from their very germ plasm.

What little remained of the gruesome masque was played out with grim inevitability. When Monroe awoke to the strident clangor of the bugle the following Sunday, he found in Norma's stead a gruff

Levantine with a blue jowl, whose busby and scarlet regimentals contrasted oddly with the cigar stump he was chewing. In a perfunctory mumble utterly devoid of esprit de corps, he rattled off the standard salutation of Yale Lox Associates and with uncouth bad grace brought forth some dismal marinated herring and salt-stengels.

Monroe blinked at him apprehensively. "Where's Norma?" he croaked in a peevish, tremulous voice he scarcely recognized as his own. A vague foreboding gripped him. "What happened to Miss Ganz?"

"Search me, Percy," returned the messenger. "We ain't responsible for your love life. Maybe she sneaked off before dawn." He gave a coarse chuckle.

"No, no," said Monroe, conscious of a sudden constriction in his windpipe. "Norma Ganz, the girl that usually delivers my breakfast."

"Never heard of her," said the other flatly. Pressure and appeals to his magnanimity went for naught; he was simply a cog in a vast mechanism, he indicated, whose hub was the potent and unapproachable Mr. Fabricant.

Momentarily expecting a phone call or other word from Norma, Monroe allowed the day to dissipate in an agony of indecision and fear. By the next afternoon, his inquietude had reached an almost unbearable pitch. In an interview with the girl's landlady, he ascertained that she had not been home for five days. It was possible she might have gone to Rochester to visit her folks, the landlady admitted, but she personally suspected foul play. Monroe at once telephoned Mr. Fabricant. The director of Yale Lox Associates proved remarkably elusive. When, after interminable evasion and subterfuge, he consented to answer, his reticence hinted that he knew more than he cared to disclose. Perhaps there was an overtone of special exigency in Monroe's appeal, for after a careful pause Mr. Fabricant grudgingly invited him to come in for a talk.

Seated in an office that would have made any Park Avenue kidney specialist sick with envy, Mr. Fabricant rested a basilisk stare on

"The African potentate expressed himself as overwhelmed by the hospitality shown him during his Manhattan visit."

Monroe and listened to his chronicle. When his caller had concluded, he shook his head pityingly. "My boy," he said, "you don't have to be ashamed of the love you bore that Norma Ganz. She had the same effect on me."

"What the hell are you using the past tense for?" Monroe asked hoarsely. "For heaven's sake, tell me the worst!"

"Hold your horses." Fabricant quieted him. "I'm in the personal-catering game nine years and it's things like this that's made an old man of me."

"Things like what?" cried Monroe. "Get the marbles out of your mouth!"

"This," said Mr. Fabricant, wearily opening a drawer and extending a newspaper cutting. Under a photograph of a gigantic Masai warrior posed with shield and spear, a silk hat on his head, and his neck encircled with lion's teeth, was the curt report that Prince Balegula had embarked for Dar es Salaam after a good-will tour of Hollywood, Washington, and New York. "The African potentate," concluded the account, "expressed himself as overwhelmed by the hospitality shown him during his Manhattan visit. Even his favorite delicacy, he said, had been forthcoming while here, and, in fact, he had not been compelled to leave his suite to enjoy it."

"It can't be," sobbed Monroe, cradling his face in his arms. "Maybe she eloped with him. I'll get the inside story."

"You got it in front of your nose, son," said Mr. Fabricant. He laid before the other a gold epaulet Monroe remembered only too well. "They found this in his kitchenette at the Waldorf after he checked out." A tear coursed down his cheek as he leaned over and patted Monroe's heaving shoulders. "Life goes on," he sighed. "We all arrive at the city of God, but some by different gates. *Lox vobiscum.*"

Be a Peacock!
Earn Big Acrimony

I RECENTLY broke bread, if so lordly a phrase may be applied to a chopped-chicken-liver sandwich, with an actor friend of mine named Pillsbury who was recovering from a pretty shattering experience. Pillsbury (unrelated to the flour people except as a consumer) is a tramp comic who, since the decline of burlesque and vaudeville, has exhibited his drolleries in musical comedy and night clubs with signal success. Not long ago, a chance presented itself to him to play that celebrated music hall, the London Palladium. Pillsbury had never appeared in England, and nursed a lifelong reverence for its traditions and culture. His equal veneration of the pound sterling, especially as deposited in a Manhattan checking account, made the opportunity an exceptional one. He jumped at it.

A day or two after sailing from New York, however, he was seized by a gnawing anxiety. As he paced the boat deck reviewing his act, he began to ask himself whether a cultivated British audience might not find his professional makeup and props too flamboyant for its taste. A public steeped in Jane Austen and Trollope, he reasoned, would hardly tolerate such robust humors as his red putty nose and imitation-diamond stickpin three inches in diameter. At a point roughly two hundred miles off the Georges Bank, after considerable mental turmoil, Pillsbury decided to dispense with them. The ship was nearing mid-ocean when he reached a similar conclusion regarding the baggy trousers he had worn for the past thirty years. It wrung his heart to part with them, but if it meant the difference between success and failure, he knew how futile it was to vacillate. The following day was reasonably peaceful, and then, toward nightfall, the thought of his outsize shoes and towering celluloid collar started to

132

plague him. They were much too broad; far better eliminate them now, while there was yet time, than run the risk of being hooted off the stage. Fifteen hours from Land's End, Pillsbury made a final concession to the English temper. He abandoned the pig's bladder with which he customarily struck the conducter over the head to emphasize his points.

Six nights later, transformed from a frowzy pantaloon into the glass of fashion, Pillsbury stood in the wings of the Palladium awaiting his turn to go on, attired in a superbly cut Andersen & Sheppard dress suit and nervously shooting his cuffs. He was diligently rehearsing a set of prefatory remarks that included quotations from Lovelace, Cowper, and Alfred Noyes when there materialized next to him an extraordinary individual. The man was clad in orange-colored silk shorts, on his feet were a pair of ladies' Juliets and around his neck an Elizabethan ruff. He wore red muttonchop whiskers, and his midriff was speckled with alternate fuchsia and Nile-green dots. An intermittent electric bulb winked on and off in the crown of his brass bowler, and around its brim puffed a tiny steam train, which occasionally emitted a shrill whistle. Pillsbury gaped incredulously at the apparition for a full thirty seconds. At length, he cleared his throat.

"I — I beg your pardon," he faltered, "but who are you?"

"Me?" inquired the other with an artless smile. "Why, I'm the straight man in the act that follows you."

By an odd coincidence, I underwent an experience a few months back that, while not as unnerving as Pillsbury's, also involved peculiar apparel, interhemisphere travel, and ultimate frustration. Quietly assembling the necessary kit for a voyage along the equator, I suddenly found myself buried under an avalanche of expert advice from friends. None of them had ever been west of the Cucamonga wineries, but they knew to a shooting stick what I would require in the steaming jungles of Sumatra and the grassy uplands of Tanganyika. The requisites ranged from underwater goggles to a Pliofilm poncho, from snakeproof puttees to a Balaklava helmet. One man forced me to buy a pair of whipcord jodhpurs, despite my protestations that I was calling on the Maharajah of Jodhpur and would unquestionably receive a pair as a door prize. Another swore I would be *kaput* without a folding machete, and, sensing a slight hesitation, had one sent to me by Abercrombie's, charging it to my account. I finally rebelled when a total stranger at a cocktail party tried to bullyrag me into taking along forty gross of Mother Hubbards to trade to the Andaman Islanders. The fact that the Andamans were a penal colony and that I was neither a missionary nor a wholesaler did not interest him. He said it would be a shrewd business move.

On one point my advisers were all united, though, and that was the utter imperative necessity for a tropical dinner jacket. The stringent social code east of Suez, they assured me, made it mandatory; they painted horrifying pictures of my embarrassment while attending viceregal functions in mufti, warned me I would lose face with my bearers if, at the end of a day's trek, I lacked formal dress to change into. Eventually, I weakened and betook myself to Brooks Brothers, which has survived five wars, to say nothing of protracted litigation over my account. The salesman looked at me pityingly. Surely I must be aware of the fabulous scarcity of linen, rayon, shantung silk, gabardine, and poplaire since Pearl Harbor. I told him I had been doing a sixer on the Rock and was out of touch. He ventured to say there was not a white dinner coat to be had in the city. DePinna, Finchley, and Tripler were similarly bleak, but the last suggested that if all else failed I might pick up a mess jacket at a towel-supply house. I retorted that I did not propose to meet the Nawab of Bhopal looking like a soda dispenser. That floored them. I could see they were sorry they had ever crossed swords with *me*.

The same dolorous picture greeted me at every outfitter's I went to; I even considered renting a white jacket from a theatrical costumer for the evening and decamping with it, only to find that others had anticipated me. The one garment dimly resembling what I sought was a minstrel tuxedo worn in the *Hot Mikado*, with rhinestone buttons and lapels faced in baby-blue velveteen that flared six inches above the collar, but it was too small for me. At the eleventh hour, an old crony who had risen to head a national chain of men's shops magically came to my aid. Buzzers were pressed, teletypes invoked, and in jig time a light-weight dinner coat soared in by air express from Cleveland. The moment I saw it in the triple mirror of the alteration booth, I realized my exultation had been premature. The shoulders had been built out with football pads and the whole affair hung down to the knees, strangely foreshortening me so that I had the air of a rather alert chimpanzee. To renege was out of the question after the *brouhaha* I had caused; I did the only honorable thing under the circumstances. Requesting a fountain pen from the fitter, I accidentally joggled his arm in such wise as to stipple ink over the coat, and, thus freed of any obligation to buy it, departed with a clear conscience.

In Hollywood, where I dallied several weeks before sailing, I felt confident my search must bear fruit; the entire philosophy of the motion picture, so to speak, was predicated on the white dinner jacket. But here, again, for all the opulent toggery that crowded the haberdashers' racks — the corduroy play suits piped in vicuña and the shot-silk blazers with genuine chamois pockets — I was met with shrugs. Just as I was resigning myself to the bitter inevitability of being a pariah in the Torrid Zone, a matron moved by my plight had an inspiration. Her brother-in-law, a barber, supplemented his income by playing the traps in a five-piece combo at Monrovia. Certainly he would know any number of bandsmen willing to yield their working clothes for a consideration. An appeal was immediately broadcast, with results that were little short of spectacular. From eight o'clock onward the next morning, half the membership of Musicians' Local 47 appeared at my door, bearing coats of every size and description. They were made of piqué, twill, duck, muslin, canvas, jute, cashmere, buckram, bengaline, bobbinet, brocatel — materials I thought existed only in the overheated fancy of advertising copywriters. There was, of course, not a single white one in the lot; the eleven possibilities I set aside to choose from were all tinted deli-

. . . the whole affair hung down to the knees

cate shades, like canary, lilac, peach, and greige. The least offensive (though I was fully aware my judgment was warped by fatigue) was a mauve-colored article with two vents and a grotesque shawl collar. Its shoulders also were heavily padded, and one bore a stain where, the owner sadly informed me, a drunken starlet had shied a matzoth ball at him in the Trocadero. This could easily be camouflaged by dusting a bit of talc onto it, he said, and, swayed by his candor and an embarkation date two days off, I consummated the deal.

What with a radical change of course, wrought by dislocated steam-ship schedules, the first occasion to display my finery arose in Shanghai. The temperature was close to freezing (it was mid-March), but I was cautioned that I would be outlawed by Sir Victor Sassoon and international society generally unless I dressed for the night club atop the Cathay Hotel. Sir Victor must have taken a powder before I got there; the only social arbiters in the dark, glacial room were three Norwegian seamen clad in sweatshirts. I slipped in, trying to look as inconspicuous as possible, but the clientele quite justifiably mistook me for the floor show and applauded vigorously. Quick to adapt himself to any contingency, the band leader threw a blinding cerise spot-light on me and swung his balalaikas into "Rufus Rastus Johnson Brown, What You Goin' to Do When the Rent Comes 'Round?" I did not think that my sole parlor recitation, Senator Vest's tribute to his dog, would stir a cosmopolitan group of Scandinavians, Slavs, and Chinese singsong girls. Blushing like a peony and mumbling broken excuses, I retired into a corner, where I slowly congealed until the sight of the check thawed me out. I asked the waiter sardonically whether the tariff was steeper for men in heliotrope dinner coats, but the shaft went right over his head; he nodded. Irony is lost on these Orientals. They never get it.

Meandering down the China coast and up into Siam, I encountered no situation that cried out for formal wear until I struck Bangkok. For a while, I managed to postpone using my bird-of-paradise raiment; pretending a bold, bohemian indifference to convention, I dined out in a Windsor tie and a rumpled alpaca number I got from a side-walk vender. Then, one night, at an extremely starchy banquet at the Dutch Legation, destiny again gave me the hotfoot. Earlier in the day, my host at the American Embassy had indicated that serious political consequences, possibly even a rupture of diplomatic relations, might ensue if I attended the affair in a sack suit. I dug out the tropical jacket and tried minimizing the blotch with talc, as directed. To my dismay, it became still more pronounced — indeed, unmistakable. It occurred to me that perhaps by balancing it with a smudge on the other shoulder I could pass them off as some unusual kind of **137** epaulets. The number-one boy rustled up a bowl of gravy from the kitchen, and together we contrived an effect I was confident would be dashing, provided the lights were subdued enough.

The illusion was perfect up to the moment I entered the Netherlands Legation; in fact, as I ascended the moonlit steps, the Russian doorman, Latchky by name, gave me a cluck of approval and a crisp military salute. The Burmese major-domo dropped his tray of hors-d'œuvre when he saw me, but he may have been nervous anyway. Beyond an occasional stifled gasp as each arriving guest caught sight of me, nobody seemed to find my wardrobe out of the ordinary. The dining room, unhappily, was lit up like a surgical amphitheater, so, seated on my hostess's right, I had a clear, unobstructed view of sixteen pairs of eyes bulging from their sockets. The seventeenth, my American sponsor's, remained on his plate throughout the meal, and his lips moved silently. Conversation was on the desultory side. To lessen the tension, I launched into several anecdotes that would have slain the company had I been able to remember the nub. Nonetheless, I persisted gamely, and soon, by a sturdy espousal of Indonesian liberty, kindled the usually phlegmatic Hollanders. On the way out, I passed two British code clerks climbing into their jeep. "Well, I've seen everything now," one was saying. "Crikey, a violet dinner jacket!" "Rum go," agreed the other. "Always something different at the Dutch Legation."

I wore the coat but once more on my journey, although not, I must admit, to comparable social acclaim. It was aboard the *President Polk* in the Arabian Sea, a day distant from Aden. I was sauntering in to the captain's dinner, sleek and resplendent in my hot-weather plumage and redolent of Florida water, when a curious mishap overtook me. The chief steward intercepted me at the door and explained that the chair I always occupied had inexplicably collapsed. Inasmuch as it would take Chips, the ship's carpenter, a morning to rebuild it — the vessel was extremely short of chairs — he wondered if I would mind eating in my cabin. He became somewhat insistent about it, to tell the truth, plainly maneuvering me back to my stateroom the whole time he was talking. I objected, as might anyone, to missing the fun, but he made small of my qualms, promising I should have all the paper hats and noisemakers I wanted. After he had gone, locking the door from the outside, I began to feel a growing mistrust for his story. Either I was embroiled in a spy intrigue concerned with secret papers concealed in the chair, an unlikely theory, or the jacket had diddled me again. On the instant, an irrational disrelish for my role seized me. I was through being duped and blackguarded by another man's livery, no matter how jaunty. With one deft gesture, I stripped the jacket off and opened the porthole. The last I saw of it, it was bobbing away in the wake toward Pakistan. I don't know whether it's reached there yet, but I can tell those Muslims one thing. They think they've got *problems*. Just wait.

Pain Counterpane

IF THE EDITORS of *Life* could arrange to hush the roar of their mighty presses for a few seconds, I'd like to return their wedding ring. I have conscientiously taken in their paper ever since it was reborn eight years ago, and I'll bet my bottom dollar, which is a half inch removed from my top one, that they've never had a more patient, loyal reader. Week in, week out, I have submitted without flinching to the most chilling closeups of black widows engaged in courtship, roosters strolling composedly about the barnyard months after decapitation, and cardiac patients in valvular disarray. At a word from the editors, I have waded through Nilotic mud with staff photographers to study the hibernation of the lungfish, shinnied up the highest sierra to peer into eagles' nests, and ranged the most noisome guano islands of Chile to keep abreast of the nitrate situation. Though terrified of heights, I have gamely parachuted out of bombers at twenty-five thousand feet; a lifelong foe of ritual and mumbo jumbo, I have allowed myself to be hazed by obscure sororities in Midwestern colleges. Even when *Life's* editorials developed a pitch of chauvinism reminiscent of the late Theodore Roosevelt, I stood by mutely, although my newsdealer did cut me dead for a fortnight. Well, I suppose it was inevitable that the honeymoon would end sooner or later, but I never thought a couple of advertisements for bedclothes would do it. Fellows, I'm going home to Mother. And please don't write, because I'll just return your letters unopened.

The first note of dissonance in our idyll was the appearance, some

five months ago, of an advertisement for Pequot Sheets grimly cap-
tioned "I want to make a confession." Out of the printed page, a tear-
stained letter crushed against her bosom, there stared at me what
was intended to be a repentant housewife, mystifyingly portrayed by
a Conover model sporting a cool thousand dollars' worth of Cartier
gold-shell jewelry. Apparently, a Mrs. I. O. Siler, of Mesena, Georgia,
tortured by guilt, had sat down in a deeply penitent mood and written
a letter to the Pequot Mills, begging their forgiveness. For years,
she admitted, she had gone along thinking Pequots were too luxurious
for her purse. Then came revelation, brought by the ubiquitous friend
who turns up at this juncture with the balmier astringent, the creamier
mayonnaise, or the deadlier insecticide. She gave Mrs. Siler a pair
of Pequots and the courage to perform one of those analyses copywriters adore. "Being experimental-minded," said Mrs. Siler, "I proceeded to make a detailed comparison between those Pequots and
my lower-priced bed linens. *I found I had been cheating myself
shamefully!*" With a ringing hosanna to the durability and comfort
of Pequots, the lady thereupon signed her name in blood on the shin-
gle and pledged herself never to use any other brand. Fired by her
example, I decided to make a vow of my own. I carefully spread the
issue of *Life* in the fashion of a prayer rug, knelt down facing toward
its Eastern Circulation Department, and took a solemn oath to avoid
all future advertisements for bed linen, no matter how provocative.

But I had not counted on the forces pitted against me. Skimming
through *Life's* advertising columns several weeks back, I paused to
admire an illustration of a fetching party in flowered chiffon. Her
roguish eyes proved my undoing; a moment too late I heard the whir
of a well-oiled mechanism and I landed up to my hips in Cannon Percale Sheets. The merchandising device in this instance was a narrative as grisly as any ever confected by Bierce or Fitz-James O'Brien.
In the classified section of her newspaper, a young woman has run
across an urgent appeal by an ex-pilot and his wife for lodgings.
Moved by their plight, the young woman and her husband present
them with a spare room — a touching enough gesture until you dis-

cover it is merely a pretext for the matron to ululate endlessly about her Cannon Percales. After a few warm-up phrases, like "so blissfully practical" and "sense-making, down-to-earth prices," she really opens up on her luckless guest: "While the men swapped war records, we got down to girl-talk. . . . I gave the gal a preview — of Life With Cannon Percales! How sweet-sleeping they are. How smooth — woven of specially selected cotton so fine that every Cannon Percale Sheet has 25% more threads per inch than best-grade muslins! Then I wound up with raves about the way Cannon Percale Sheets wear and wear. I tossed in some remarks about their *lightness* — easier for bedmaking; easier to wash. And signed off with a reminder just to look for that Cannon label, come the day of setting up real housekeeping!"

Although such diverse plays as *Trilby* and *Kind Lady* have successfully exploited the theme of the dominant personality who grafts his will upon that of a weakling, this is the first time to my knowledge that it has cropped up in the drygoods field. While no *Angel Street*, the dilemma of two unfortunates in the toils of a woman fixated on bed linen has traces of taut melodrama. So taut, in fact, that I feel it my duty to offer a few of them in handy, dehydrated form to any Broadway showman with room on his fall schedule for a fast, inexpensive failure.

> SCENE: *The spare bedroom of the Sprackling family, a comfortably furnished chamber. At rise, Mrs. Sprackling, a bright, birdlike woman of thirty, is smoothing the wrinkles from the sheets on the twin beds while Viola and Pascal Budlong, a young couple, look on miserably, half dead with fatigue.*

MRS. SPRACKLING (*crooning to the sheets*): Aren't these Sandman Superdupercales the most inviting things you ever saw? Just look at them!

PASCAL: That's what I've been doing for the last three hours.

MRS. SPRACKLING: You remind me of my husband. Sometimes he never goes to bed at all; he just sits up all night admiring their snowy sheen.

VIOLA: We'd like to do that, too, Mrs. Sprackling, but it's almost two-thirty and Pascal here has to get up at seven.

MRS. SPRACKLING: Of course he does, poor lamb. But don't you fret, an hour's rest between Sandmans is equivalent to eight between ordinary sheets. That's because they're Gossamerized, you know. A secret patented process seals special health-stimulating chemicals into every tiny pore of the fabric. Ask any laundryman.

PASCAL (*desperately*): I will. I'll stop in at the Chinaman's first thing tomorrow.

MRS. SPRACKLING: Get him to unravel a few strands of Sandman and roll them between his fingers. Then examine those fingers. You won't find any of the grit and abrasives associated with lower-priced brands.

PASCAL: I'm sure I won't. Well, good night now, Mrs. Sprackling.

MRS. SPRACKLING (*lingering*): Somehow, I don't feel right abandoning you this way. Are you sure you two have everything you need?

VIOLA: Oh, absolutely. It's mighty sweet of you to take us in.

MRS. SPRACKLING: Nonsense. How about some fresh sheets on the beds, while I'm here?

VIOLA (*faintly*): But you've changed them three times so far this evening.

MRS. SPRACKLING: It won't take a second. I always keep a large economy package of Sandman Superdupercales in the closet should unexpected guests arrive. (*She backs hastily toward the door as Pascal begins removing his trousers.*) Would you like a magazine or anything to read?

VIOLA: No, thanks. We're both pretty bushed.

MRS. SPRACKLING: In case you're looking for something, there's a perfectly fascinating booklet on the night table, put out by the Sandman people. It's full of real-life stories of folks who got into trouble using other makes of sheets.

VIOLA: I — I'll dip into it.

MRS. SPRACKLING: And whatever you do, don't miss the part about their comprehensive insurance plan. For only twenty dollars a month, they send you a coupon entitling you to a five-per-cent discount on any new Sandman Superdupercales you buy. It amounts to a generous saving in the course of a year. See you later! (*She goes. Viola collapses, face buried in her hands.*)

PASCAL (*impatiently*): Listen, there's no time for sniveling. We've got to think our way out of this!

VIOLA (*moaning*): I — I can't. I feel numb all over.

PASCAL: It's only a little slogan poisoning. You'll be O.K. in a minute.

VIOLA: If I could just creep into bed for a while . . . it's so soft . . .

PASCAL (*wrenching her away*): No, no, you mustn't give in! Keep moving — flap your arms. (*He scrabbles frantically in a suitcase, extracts a Consumer's Research bulletin, which he presses to her nose. Her eyes focus.*) There — how's that?

VIOLA: M-m-m, better . . . lots better.

PASCAL: Good. Now, quick! Close the bags while I knot these sheets together.

VIOLA: What are we going to do?

PASCAL: Take the only avenue of escape left open to us.

VIOLA: You mean the window?

PASCAL: Yes. Fortunately, the scenic designer had the presence of mind to include one in this set. (*He has fastened their impromptu lifeline to the radiator when a soft knock is heard.*)

MRS. SPRACKLING (*through door*): Oh, Mrs. Budlong! Are you asleep?

VIOLA (*tensely*): What'll I say?

PASCAL: Anything! Build it up!

VIOLA (*raising her voice*): Asleep, did you ask? Who wouldn't be, with the Sandman trademark supervising every aching nerve?

PASCAL (*also fortissimo*): Yes, sirree, and while we're on it, we fussy males sure appreciate their added full-fashioned width! No tossing and turning, no irritating tussle with *my* bed coverings. Boy, oh, boy!

MRS. SPRACKLING: You're not asleep — I can see you moving around through the keyhole!

VIOLA: She's coming in!

PASCAL: Get into bed and pull this pillowcase over your head!

VIOLA: What for?

He trusses her up, anchors her firmly to a bedpost.

PASCAL: Never mind — do as I tell you! (*He crosses to door, admits Mrs. Sprackling, her arms laden with sheets.*)

MRS. SPRACKLING: I just couldn't rest worrying about you children. I've brought you some extra — Good heavens, what's wrong with your wife?

PASCAL: Why, nothing. She always sleeps that way.

MRS. SPRACKLING: How can she breathe inside there?

PASCAL: I'm glad you asked that question, Mrs. Sprackling. Recent experiments conducted by an impartial jury of America's foremost diagnosticians conclusively establish that Sandman's High-Porosity Pillowcases filter out deleterious particles in the night air and ensure a restful, zestful slumber.

MRS. SPRACKLING: I never knew that.

PASCAL: You didn't? Then, why delay? Why not follow the example of millions of American women and make this new, exciting test for yourself? (*He strips off a pillowcase, advances on her.*)

MRS. SPRACKLING: Wait — I'd like to think it over — consult my husband —

PASCAL: Skeptical, eh? Full of doubts, hard to satisfy? You'll cry fie to substitutes once you've enjoyed Sandman's Five-Way, All-Purpose Bean Bag. Hey, Presto! (*He trusses her up, anchors her firmly to a bedpost.*)

VIOLA: Do you think she'll be all right like that?

PASCAL: Oh, yes, unless, of course, something unforeseen ensues, such as a sudden apoplectic seizure.

VIOLA: That might prove extremely embarrassing for us, dear.

PASCAL: Now, lover, let's not cross that bridge until we come to it. (*He helps her over the window sill as Mrs. Sprackling methodically begins to gnaw her way to freedom.*)

CURTAIN

Strictly from Mars, or, How to Philander in Five Easy Colors

S OME LOVE Van Johnson, some van Gogh; for every youth who pins up a photograph of Alexis Smith, there is another who does the same for Betty. Sneer if you will at the veal-faced adolescent haunting Grand Central for a glimpse of Perry Como; one of these evenings you will claw your way through the lobby at a first-night intermission to genuflect before Evelyn Waugh or Shostakovitch. Everyone, no matter how case-hardened, has his joss. I know a poised and cultivated woman whose contempt for her husband is infinite because he spent two years maneuvering an introduction to Bill Dickey. Last summer, she crouched for a whole afternoon in a bog on Martha's Vineyard to beg an autograph of Katharine Cornell. I, too, have my idol, and if he is neither toreador nor tenor, philosopher nor clown, he is nonetheless romantic for being a plain businessman. Paradoxically enough, I have never heard his name, and I wouldn't be at all sure he exists, except for the indisputable evidence of his handiwork. He is the man who dreams up the dialogue in those advertising comic strips.

The general story pattern of these strips, while elementary, has the rugged simplicity of a piece of pre-Columbian sculpture or the Jupiter Symphony. The hero, a small boy or a creature from outer space, stumbles on various simple or compound disasters and averts them through superhuman strength derived from eating a given cereal or sandwich spread. Though never conveyed in so many words, there is usually a sly implication that the purchaser will acquire similar prowess the instant he lays his money on the barrelhead.

A convenient specimen appeared in a recent Sunday *Herald Tribune*. It shows Peter Pan, a strangely mammiferous teen-ager in a Lincoln green jerkin, stepping out of the trademark on a jar of peanut butter and beguiling a boy to the circus. The pair breathlessly watches the star trapeze act, in which a girl aerialist shuttles between her own flimsy perch and the hands of her catcher. Suddenly, a rope frays and the girl dangles perilously beyond the catcher's reach. "Hang on!" encourages the ringmaster, who evidently has seen peanut butter save the day in many a crisis. "Peter Pan's on the way!" His faith is vindicated forthwith, when Peter swings out and snatches the girl, her ankles gripped by the catcher, back to safety. "Thanks for saving my life, Peter Pan," the latter observes somewhat lymphatically. "Yes," adds the ringmaster, a man obviously accustomed to deal with any social situation. "And I'm treating everybody to these swell peanut-butter sandwiches. Take all you want, folks!" By my limited standards, such munificence is roughly synonymous with a left to the kidneys, but circus people have their own curious code. With the final terse announcement *"It does not stick to the roof of your mouth!,"* Peter Pan steps back in the label and the reader presumably rushes to the nearest grocer. I started to, but my head was wedged between a couple of sofa pillows, and as it would have meant cutting it away with an acetylene torch, I decided to string out the autumn on margarine.

"How Thom McAn Foiled the Flood," a strip decorating the back cover of a comic book called *Wonder Woman*, also has its moments of rare verbal beauty. Thom, a red-headed lad of Herculean vitality, is introduced lounging with three friends "outside the clubhouse of the Thom McAn Shoes-True Pals," surely the most neuralgic collection of words ever yoked together in English. Informed by a radio flash that the town dam has broken, he hastily dons a pair of weird red Juliets, which he refers to as "bazooka-shoes," and whizzes to the scene. "Wow!" he shudders as he sees the torrent about to engulf the town. "Not a second to spare! And I can't move the town — so I have to move the flood!" Employing his shoes as a bulldozer, Thom rips a channel through the mountain, thus enabling the river to by-pass the town, and returns to the club to receive the plaudits of his friends. "These 'bazooka-shoes' are O.K. for emergencies," he comments wryly. "But for everyday comfort and fun, I'll take good ol' Thom McAn shoes!" His jubilant comrades suggest a feast to celebrate his exploit, but Thom suddenly stands on protocol: "Wait, Jimmy here can't enter. He's not 'shoe-true to Thom McAn!'" After humiliating Jimmy so thoroughly that they lay the foundation for a whopping psychic trauma, his chums agree to let the outlaw participate, on condition he dig up a pair of Thom McAns. An hour later, Thom greets him at the clubhouse door. "Enter, pal," he says with greasy affability. "Your shoes are the key. Now you are officially a 'Thom McAn Shoe-True Pal!'" This piquant hash of child psychology and salesmanship, incidentally, appeared in a publication whose advisory board includes an assistant professor of education at Columbia, a professor of psychiatry and one of English literature at New York University, Pearl Buck, and Gene Tunney. The names Captain Bligh and Torquemada were missing from the masthead. I guess they happened to be out of town.

The most captivating example of this sort of moonshine I have met, however, is the strip called "Volto, He Comes from Mars Possessing Strange Magnetic Powers!," in a journal named *Star Spangled Comics,* which I found stashed in my son's bed a few days ago. We first encounter Volto, an interplanetary version of the late Lou Tellegen, on a roller coaster with a small boy. Suddenly, down the incline toward them hurtles another car. "What a way to run a roller coaster!" exclaims Volto pettishly. "I better get busy!" He extends his left hand, repelling the car, but the ensuing jolt dislodges one of the passengers, a reasonably well-stacked brunette. As she falls headlong, Volto extends his right hand and she is magically swept into his arms. A concessionaire hurries up to offer Volto a hundred dollars for the secret of his stunt. "It's no trick for Volto!" announces his young companion. "He's from Mars, where everybody gets that magnetism from eating whole-grain cereals!" Volto, plainly reluctant, looses his hold on the **149** maiden. "And I must have some right now to recharge my power!" he chimes in with a wolfish grin. Simpering, the brunette tucks back a stray wisp of hair. "Then," she proposes, "let me repay you with the tastiest whole-grain cereal in this world — Grape-Nuts Flakes!" In the final tableau, Volto has apparently whisked the girl away to a quiet little cafeteria for a few rounds of flakes, and the strip concludes with the boy exalting the virtues of the cereal.

An electric climax to a thrilling episode — and yet, somehow, the whole affair leaves one chopfallen. What *did* become of Volto and his little pigeon after they left the park? What about Volto's home life — did Mrs. Volto know where he was? Why was he bumming around an amusement park on Earth when he should have been tending to business on Mars? Obviously, Grape-Nuts is playing its cards very close to the vest indeed, and if we are to have an explanation, we shall have to evolve it ourselves. I'll go first:

Alice Volto stirred sleepily on her chaise longue, her ear cocked at the sound of her husband's tread in the corridor. She heard him fumble unsteadily at the keyhole; after a moment the door slammed and a penetrating odor of oatmeal wafted out of the foyer, punctuated by a stifled belch. "Oh, damnation," she thought hopelessly. "Another toot. And after all his promises, too." She held up her wrist watch to the back of her head, where the best of her eyes was located, and peered at the time. Nine-fifteen — two hours late. He would probably have some overplausible yarn about being detained by a client from Betelgeuse or Charles's Wain. She arose with weary resignation, flicked a suède buffer across her nose to accent its patrician metallic gleam, and issued into the living room.

"Hi, sweet," Volto mumbled from behind his evening paper. He was aware that he was holding it upside down, but he didn't care; he felt ghastly. If only he hadn't let that little tramp cajole him into a final dish of Crispies.

"Everything all right at the office?" asked Alice, casually levitating herself to the mantelpiece and lighting a cigarette. She had long since learned the value of forbearance and cunning with her husband.

"Oh, tiptop!" said Volto, assuming a grimace intended to convey sunny insouciance. "I blew out a sprocket this morning, but the nurse at the infirmary welded it."

"Better stop around at the plumber's in the morning and have a checkup," his wife advised. "You may still have a little steam in your gauge from last winter."

"No, I — I feel great," Volto assured her, nimbly brushing an ashtray to the floor and strewing the rug with butts. His red-lacquered neck turned a deeper shade. Alice, her lip curling in amused contempt, extended her right hand and the ashtray leaped back to the table. In the short, meaningful silence that followed, a fine perspiration mantled her husband's forehead.

"You must be famished, darling," remarked Alice, at last. "Your dinner's in the alcove."

"Why — er — uh, I don't think I want anything right now," said Volto, with a sickly grin. "I had a rather late lunch —"

"But it's your favorite dish!" Alice objected. "I made you a great big bowl of Wheaties mixed with Kix and shredded bran. You adore it."

"I know," Volto admitted unhappily. "But you see, I — well, this small goy I met on the midway — er, I mean to say *boy* —"

"What midway?" Alice interrupted.

"Why the amusement park," he faltered. "The one down there on the Earth. Say, you wouldn't believe the way they run their roller coasters! Irresponsible — yes, sir, absolutely insane!"

"Really?" Alice's voice abruptly turned glacial. "What were you doing on the roller coaster?"

"Who, me?" asked Volto innocently. "Nothing. I was just riding in the front seat with this boy."

"I thought you were at the office all afternoon," said Alice.

"What's the matter with you — don't you understand Martian?" shouted Volto. "I told you I was down on Earth, didn't I?"

"I'm sorry," said Alice. "Well, go on."

"I *am* going on!" he screamed. "Only, for God's sake, stop yelling 'Go on, go on' at me! It's enough to drive a man crazy." He paused, drew some steel wool from his pocket, and sponged his brow. "Well, we were zooming along like anything, when a girl fell out of the other car —"

"Oh," said Alice. "Was she pretty?"

"What's that got to do with it?" demanded Volto savagely.

"Nothing," said Alice. "I was just curious."

"Well, don't start reading double meanings into everything," snapped her husband. "When I see a party in mortal peril, I don't ask if they're a Conover model before I go to their aid."

"No, but it comes in handy afterward," commented Alice. "What happened then?"

"Nothing," replied Volto. "I used my strange magnetic powers, that's all."

"I bet you did," said his wife. "Was she grateful?"

"How do you mean?" asked Volto cautiously.

"Well, you saved her life, if I interpret your story correctly."

"Too damn grateful," returned Volto. "You never saw such a nuisance. I wanted to come home, but she made me go and have some whole-grain cereals with her."

"Where — in a restaurant?" inquired Alice.

"Well — uh, not exactly." Volto hesitated. "You see, all the restaurants down there close by three in the afternoon. We tried 'em."

"But then she remembered she had some cereal up at her place, I suppose," suggested Alice.

"Why, how did you know?" asked Volto, taken aback.

"Oh, I just guessed," smiled his wife. "I always kept some on hand for emergencies before I knew you."

"Well, it was pretty white of her, all the same," said Volto defensively. "If I hadn't found some way to recharge, I might never have come back to this planet."

"My goodness," said Alice with a certain degree of composure. "Whatever would have become of me?"

"I thought you were at the office all afternoon," said Alice.

"That's what I was afraid of," explained Volto. "It had me plenty worried for a spell."

"Well, dear," said Alice, descending from her perch, "you've had a full day, haven't you? Why don't you run along to bed?"

"Think I will," yawned her husband. "You going to sit up and read awhile?"

"No, I believe I'll take a spin," said Alice thoughtfully. "Did you leave the rocket out?"

Volto nodded. "Going over to your mother's?" he asked.

"Uh-uh," smiled Alice. "Coney Island."

Next Thurs- (Mar 7) Greensleeves. 7:30 | Dolly's

* " Sat (9) (Mar) " 8 (increase by 2) |
  Sugar Cane Club -10 7:30 — Sat 9.
✓ This Sat (2) (Mar) Dolly . 7:30
  " Thurs Bagatelle 8:30
  Feb 28

Sat Mar 9
Reserv. - for 10- Sugar Cane Club.
  " 8- Greensleeves

Thurs - March 7th - 22321 - Grotto
  7:30 -

Cancel - Sugar cane for Mar 9.
Call Greensleeves for Thurs- Mar 7- for 8 -